Christy,

I'm 52 years old now and all I can say about your presentation is this; "only If" all those theapists & counselors would have educated me beginning at 12 years old — it wouldnt have taken most of my life to get it Right.

I've been saying educate these youth on the subjects of trauma before, during, and after their treatments ☺ IN MY Keys for 3 years!

God Bless You!

Paula

I would love to hear your reviews! Please email me at: edgeofunthinkable@yahoo.com or visit my website at www. edgeofunthinkable.com

On the Edge of

Unthinkable

The memoir of

Paula Ann Kyle

iUniverse, Inc.
Bloomington

On the Edge of Unthinkable

iUniverse books may be ordered through booksellers or by contacting:
iUniverse
1663 Liberty Drive
Bloomington, IN 47403
www.iuniverse.com
1-800-Authors (1-800-288-4677)

ISBN: 978-1-4620-6806-7 (sc)
ISBN: 978-1-4620-6808-1 (e)
ISBN: 978-1-4620-6807-4 (dj)

Library of Congress Control Number: 2011961459

Printed in the United States of America

iUniverse rev. date: 12/23/2011

This memoir, *On the Edge of Unthinkable*, is dedicated to Judith Goodhand.

Visit with Judith in 2007

On the Edge of Unthinkable
Praise

Without better foster parents, we will *never* have better outcomes for foster kids. Speaking as a former foster child myself, I've noticed that many current foster parents want a "road map" regarding how to be the best foster parents possible. Thank you, Paula, for giving it to them.

Lisa Dickson, Founder and Communications Chair,
Ohio chapter of Foster Care Alumni of America,
www.fcaa-oh.org

Having Paula Kyle share her personal journey through the foster-care system of Knox County, Ohio, with my social work students was one of the most significant class sessions of the semester. Paula told her story from the voice of her twelve-year-old self, transporting each student back to the day Paula and her sisters walked up their driveway to meet their caseworkers and to face the realization that their family would be separated forever. Paula's transparency brought many students to tears and inspired every student to believe that in the midst of adversity there is hope.

Trudy Singletary, MSW, Assistant Professor of Social Work,
Mount Vernon Nazarene University

Paula has an incredible story to share with people about her life as a child in the foster-care system. With great clarity, she takes us into the system she had to maneuver as a lost child, and her truly heroic attempts to find her siblings brought tears to my eyes. She reminds us that the human spirit is not easily quenched, that one kind word can give hope needed for a child's survival, and she holds all of us accountable for how we look at and treat our children. I would highly recommend this book to people interested in becoming foster parents, to college students who are studying social work, and to parents—sometimes we don't know what we do to those we love.

Jeanette TFW Pelton,
MSW Licensed Institute Social Worker

What an interesting and intensely personal account. I really could not put this book down, as it told of systems and events so close to my home (since I grew up in Knox County and later knew Judith Goodhand. I worked as a school psychologist in the '70s, in Knox County). Experiencing the foster-care system, as seen through Paula's eyes, consists of very touching memories, as well as agonizing ones. Her struggles were amazing. I have read many books on abuse and neglect over the years, but this one struck a chord [because I knew] some of the people. Her will to survive through things no child should have to experience (and her eventual growth and adjustment), with help from Judith, her adoptive family, and others, made this book worth reading.

Carol Detmer, Special Education Consultant,
Northern Kentucky Special Education Cooperative, 2009

Reading this story was very difficult at times. Many times I wanted to put the book away, but then I was drawn back to it, wanting to know the outcome. This is a story that anyone who works with children, in any capacity, should read. I recommend this book as reading literature for any childhood education course. When I began my teaching career in 1974, I was not prepared to deal with children who were abused or neglected in any way. Over the years, the schools have made teachers much more aware of the signs [that] should be acted upon immediately. While reading this memoir, I read words from Paula that made me look back over the course of thirty-five years [and] wonder how many signs of neglect I overlooked out of not being trained to notice. This made me very sad. I have called on Children's Services many times to look into situations where I felt something was drastically wrong. In fact, the last day of my teaching career I had to call them concerning a child in my class. I applaud Paula for wanting to get the word out about foster children and foster care. Thank goodness there are many kind families who will open their homes to children in need. I know writing this has been very difficult for her, but it is truly an amazing story.

Jan Hawkins, retired School Teacher,
Mount Vernon, Ohio

I cannot remember a time when Bonnie Ulrey's influence in matters of faith, and a practical application of that faith in life, did not have a positive effect on my choices and decisions as a young wife and mother. Bonnie's outreach into her community was varied and widespread. She volunteered many hours to enterprises of faith and to nonprofit organizations. She was a good sounding board for serious issues and had a great sense of humor, with a twinkle in her beautiful eyes. Though she was looking forward to Larry's retirement years, having raised four children of their own, it was no surprise to me when she ultimately chose to fit in with her husband's desire that they become foster parents. I do not think Bonnie ever saw a need that she did not try to meet, or ever shrank from a task that others would find daunting. She and Larry believed in the value of each life and looked well to the welfare of others. Paula's account of all that she and her sisters suffered was shocking and heartbreaking. They were *survivors* and *overcomers*! The sincere efforts made by their social workers, and the readiness of Larry and Bonnie Ulrey to take responsibility for Paula's future, offering the same aid to Sharon and Terry, was the necessary link leading to "life and that more abundant" that we would all desire. The delight is ours; the legacy is theirs!

Jolene M. Stulka, retired Executive Director,
Knox County Interchurch Social Services

It was a pleasure to have Paula Kyle visit my U.S. Literature class and introduce her book, *On the Edge of Unthinkable*. Paula's story is compelling, and her presentation is very moving. The students seemed anxious to begin reading the book, which was somewhat of a surprise to me, since many of them are reluctant readers who read below grade level. When I assigned the first chapters of the book, I fully expected to get the usual comments, such as, "Do we have to read this book?"; "Will you read it to us?"; "It looks boring!" etc., but instead, the students began reading immediately and read in absolute silence the entire fifty-minute class period! I was both pleased and surprised. This is a great book for raising awareness about the plight of foster care, and I would especially recommend it for at-risk students and reluctant readers.

Rita Dailey, English Department Chair,
Mount Vernon Senior High School, Mount Vernon Ohio

Contents

Preface...7

Chapter 1: *A Bittersweet Good-bye*....................9

Chapter 2: *Dave and Dottie* 15

Chapter 3: *Dad's Return* 21

Chapter 4: *A New Hell* 35

Chapter 5: *The Journey to New Homes*................49

Chapter 6: *God-Sent*..55

Chapter 7: *Troubled Teenager* 63

Chapter 8: *Meeting Bob* 71

Chapter 9: *Independence* 79

Chapter 10: *Twice Bitten* 91

Chapter 11: *Loss of an Angel* 115

Chapter 12: *Picking up the Pieces* 121

Chapter 13: *Paula's Reflections*.............................129

Chapter 14: *The Final Reach*................................137

Chapter 15: *Larry Remembers* 141

Chapter 16: *Christina Ann Remembers*..................149

Chapter 17: *Hundreds of Miles and Rose Bud*........161

Acknowledgments 181

Preface

In 1986, at the age of twenty-five, I was strongly encouraged to write my story, by the very admirable Judith Goodhand. Judith was the director of the Knox County, Ohio, children services agency where, in 1974, my two sisters and I were placed into the foster-care system. We were abruptly separated in October of 1974 and became wards of the state of Ohio by the end of our first year in the Ohio foster-care system. Judith was the one who was informed by our father Dave that we were no longer wanted. She has since retired after a venerable career as a director of county child protection agencies; where she has been a long-time advocate for children. She has become a lecturer around the country and has already told my story, but now it is time for me to do so. By the time Judith suggested I write my story, I was married, with an eight-year-old daughter, Christina, and a four-year-old son, Adam. I was intrigued with the idea, but I also heard the little girl inside me screaming, "No! Leave it alone!" The telling has been at times bittersweet, filled with tears and fears, but once I had opened the masterfully taped boxes of my soul, one line at a time, it began to heal me. While this story is from my perspective, it cannot be told without the contribution of my my daughter, my brother, Rick, and my foster father, Larry. I received much resistance when I requested they write a chapter each. After all, this subject was too hard for us to talk about with each other, let alone to the world. But after much soul-searching and many tears, they were able to put feelings to paper and begin the healing process. As my story is now told, I hope you, the reader, will take this message with you. Even though this began as a story about three sisters being abused, neglected, and eventually abruptly separated, it is also my story of a foster-care system that ultimately saved our lives and continues to save children's lives today. This is a work of nonfiction. The events and experiences detailed herein are all true and have been faithfully rendered, as I have remembered them, to the best of my ability. Some names, identities, and circumstances have been changed in order to protect the integrity and/or anonymity of the various individuals involved. Though conversations and events come from my keen recollection of them, they are not written to factually represent these events. I have retold them in a way that portrays the real feeling and meaning of what was said and done, in keeping with the true reality of the mood and spirit of the event. I did not tell my sisters' stories, as I believe they have the right to tell their own stories if they choose to do so.

Chapter 1
A Bittersweet Good-bye

I was just twelve years old and still mourning the death of my mother a little over a year before, when I found myself riding down the road in a stranger's car, to another stranger's house. I thought back to the night before, when, in one loveless announcement, my father had revealed that he was just "Dave" and no longer my dad. Freshly torn from the arms of my sisters, I was now heading for this place called a foster home. Anything would have to be better than the past year I had endured with my stepmom, Lynn.

Life was finally going to change. It could not get much worse. I was so glad to escape the torture of Lynn and her awful games. Now she would not be able to hit me, say horrible things to me, or force me to speak awful lies about my mother. I would also no longer have to witness her beating the twins. I was the big sister to four and felt the responsibility to keep the younger girls safe, but I could not help them now. I was consumed with guilt, knowing that Debbie and Deon, my six-year-old twin sisters, had been left behind to endure more beatings and torture by the woman we called Mrs. Hell.

During Lynn's explosions, I had prayed that God would let the girls live. I had become quite good at diverting her attention and making her hateful beatings come at me, so my sisters had a chance to escape her rage. What would she do to them now that I was leaving, and no one was there to be a decoy? My older brother, Rick, had gone back to live with his mom the night before, and my other sisters, Terry and Sharon, were being taken away with their respective caseworkers, just as I was. I held my breath, afraid to make any sound, as the cars disappeared in the distance. The thought *This is how it is to be alone* kept rolling through my mind like an out-of-control roller coaster. I had never been without my sisters before this dreadful moment. My heart was beating so fast I was getting lightheaded, and my face was blotched with redness as I tried to stop the angry tears from falling. The lady in the front seat kept asking if I was okay as she watched me in the rear-view mirror, but I refused to talk to her. I felt like hanging my head out of the car window and throwing up.

Less than an hour ago, we three older sisters—Terry, age eleven; Sharon, who was ten; and I, age twelve—had left the Mount Vernon, Ohio, middle school and boarded the bus for our thirty-minute ride home. We could only make eye contact with each other, because we did not know how to talk about what was happening in our family. It was unimaginable—we had hoped it was a nightmare or a bad joke and Dad would change his mind. But he never joked. He always said what he meant. Soon we found out it had never been more true.

We squeezed together in one green vinyl bus seat, shoulders pressed together and elbows locked, and heard only silence, in spite of all the noisy kids; our friends did not know anything was wrong. It was unthinkable to speak about it, much less remember all the moments that had taken place in a little over a year with Mrs. Hell. It was even harder to think about the next hour, when we would walk our last walk down this drive we knew as home, stand beside each other for the last time as sisters, and watch as each of the older sisters boarded strange cars heading for this odd concept of foster homes—as our younger twin sisters watched us leave them behind with Mrs. Hell.

How can they do this, and how do I stop it? Is it even possible? My mind raced, trying to find a plan to get out of this nightmare. It became a sudden, daunting reality that there was nothing I could do to stop this. The bright, crisp autumn sun that was shining that day was clouded over by a bizarre darkness. The out-of-control thoughts and feelings were tearing through my heart and soul like lightning, and I felt myself becoming physically ill. I was going mad just trying to imagine how this separation would unfold. I could only sort out one thought, which made no sense at all—I was about to lose all of my sisters.

Most of my classmates no longer asked about the bruises or why my eyes were swollen, because I had made up so many stories in the past to explain the marks that they and my teachers now assumed I was just an active and accident-prone child.

The driver turned on the flashing safety lights and pulled to a stop. The air brakes made a loud, squishy squeal, and the bifold door opened, signaling that it was time for us to get off.

We had a short walk up a hill and around a corner before we could see our house. As we approached the top of the hill, we locked elbows and grabbed hold of each other's hands. The man we had called Dad all these years had done exactly what he'd said last night he was going to do. The walk up the first knoll of the road was slow. What should have taken us about two minutes to the top took a grueling twenty. We held each other's hands, as we slowly walked up to the corner. We were totally silent in what would be our last walk together toward what we knew as home. As we approached the top of the hill, to turn the corner to see our house, we could see the driveway was filled with three unfamiliar cars. Three unfamiliar women stood with their arms crossed. They were looking down the hill at us as if we were hunted animals, finally discovered, and soon to be in captivity.

We knew our lives would never be the same again. Our silence turned into sobs, as we hugged each other, not wanting to move any closer to our house or the three strangers. Standing behind the ladies were Dad and Lynn, both sporting smug expressions. Terry leaned over and told me that she had overheard Lynn giving Dad a choice: "Either the three girls, or me." This started an instant boiling rage through me, adding to the horror of being minutes away from being separated from my sisters. The emotions that bolted through me made me feel as if I were going to explode. Hearts pounding and our eyes full of tears, we saw the cars and strangers waiting to greet us become a blur in the distance. Reluctantly we made our way down the drive, but Dad and Lynn stopped us from entering the driveway and banned the twins from coming out of the garage to say good-bye. We three were made to stand at the foot of the driveway, like criminals. Not only were we kept from sharing a parting hug with the twins, but we were not even allowed to hug each other! All we could do was share looks of hopelessness and despair.

On the driveway, next to Lynn, were three brown grocery sacks with the tops rolled down. The sacks contained the few things Lynn had gathered from our rooms, the only belongings with which we'd embark on our new lives. From the grocery sacks, one by one, Lynn pulled our diaries and read out loud, emphasizing each ugly remark we had ever written about her. She had given us the diaries as gifts months earlier. They had been a place for us to release our private thoughts and feelings, while we struggled through the loss of our mother, but we had never suspected she would broadcast their contents the way she was doing now. She wanted to make sure Dad did not have any second thoughts about sending us away, and she was sure this display would seal the decision. She proceeded with her ranting in front of the caseworkers, who politely listened but did not stop her—I think because they did not want to cause any further delay or disruption in placing us in the new homes. They just let her have her say until she ran out of steam.

After Lynn settled down, it became a sharp reality that the three cars and the three ladies attached to them were there for the purpose of separating and transporting us neatly to three separate homes. Dad told us that we would be separated because "the three of you together are more evil than any ordinary set of foster parents could be expected to supervise." One at a time, each caseworker called out the name of the child she would be taking. Debbie, one of the twins, and the little rebel of the two, ran out of the garage and pushed her way to the car I was climbing into. She had tears streaming down her face, and in a choked voice she asked if I would ever come back. She reached up and handed me a small mirror; she said it was a present and not to forget her. On the back of the mirror was an image of Jesus, holding a staff while standing in a flock of lambs. I was sure Debbie would get a beating for coming out of the garage. She ran back into the garage and stood by Deon. They both waved as long as they could before Dad and Lynn ushered them back into the house. The twins were too young to have a full understanding of what was happening to all of us as sisters. We had all lost our mother, our brother, our father, and now each other as sisters.

Dottie, Sharon, Paula, Terry, and Rick visiting family in Ohio before new base move.

Chapter 2
Dave and Dottie

My dad stood six feet four inches tall, with green eyes and reddish-blond hair. He was a very striking, clean-cut military man. I remember the blond hair on his arms the most. It was thick and curly, and we kids all played with it. He started every day with a shower, shave, and of course, very clean and pressed clothes. He shined his boots each morning before putting them on, while drinking his heavily creamed coffee and smoking his unfiltered Camel cigarettes. His routine was exact.

When I was four or five, I got up every morning before any of my other siblings, to watch him put on his uniform. He always chuckled when I came running out to watch. Sometimes I got to his boots first, so when he came out to put them on, I could help by handing him the little stretchy bands that he wore around his pant legs to keep them tucked in. He seemed to really like it when I assisted him. I felt a separate, warm closeness with Dad. He was a man of few words and mostly sober expressions. But when he spoke an order, we learned to never give him a reason to say it twice. We did what we were told and did it right away, because he was never afraid to punish us if he thought we needed it.

When we began school, he showed us how to put our clothes in order for the next school day. They were always clean and pressed. When we learned that routine, he taught us how to iron a whole weeks' worth of school clothes. He taught this with a heavy hand. It became our routine to do ironing on Sunday afternoons, and on Sunday evening he would inspect all five outfits to make sure they matched and that they were ironed correctly. Like a drill sergeant, he taught us to clean our bedrooms. He showed us how he wanted it done, and then, after we finished, he inspected our work. Every Saturday we had inspections under the beds and in the drawers and closets. If anything was out of order, he dumped everything into the middle of the room in a huge pile, and we had to start over. Sometimes it took a whole day to get it right. This was the way it was with each of our chores—and we had more chores than the average children.

During this period of our life with Dad, he was military-strict, but when he knew we needed some attention, he was there. He wrestled with us, threw us up and down or onto the bunk beds, and we would laugh and laugh until we could not catch our breath. He used to take us to the river, where he threw us out into the deep water and taught us to swim. Afterward, he would take us out for ice cream. Our life was typical of other military families; we moved frequently to different army bases. When I was six, we moved from Colorado Springs, Colorado, to El Paso, Texas. We were stationed at Fort Bliss Army Base. There was my brother, Rick, who was eight; me, six; Terry, five; and Sharon, who was four.

Two weeks later, when we barely had our things unpacked from Colorado Springs, Dad was called to serve his second tour in the Vietnam War. I remember the car ride to take him to the airport, the look on my mother's face, and how she watched him walk away down the terminal. Mostly, I remember her tears. For the next year we would be without our dad. Three months after Dad left, my mother found out she was pregnant.

My mother, Dorothy Jane Chandler, or "Dottie," was five feet two inches tall, with shiny dark hair and the greenest eyes you have ever seen. Dad used to tease her, telling her that her eyes glowed in the dark like a cat's. Her father was a full-blooded Indian (they think Apache), and in the winter Mama's skin would be as white as snow. In the summer, the army wives would put on a competition to see who could get the darkest. My mother would shock them all and win that contest every summer.

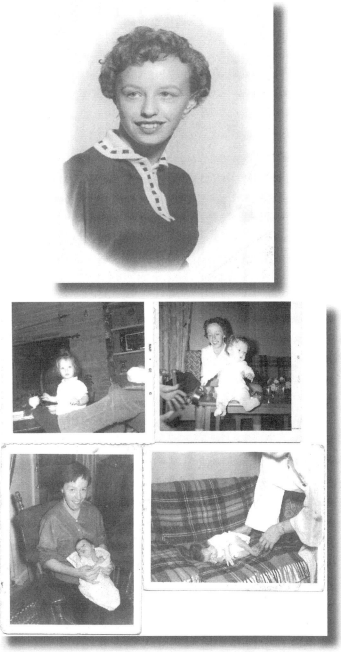

Dottie and Paula as a baby and toddler

We did not know much about Mama's birth family, nor had we ever met them. We did know that our Grandfather Chandler (the Indian) had passed away when Mama was around twenty-seven years old. While in El Paso, we gathered in groups at the army base every day with the other children of the war, waiting to learn the status of husbands and fathers. Death was all around us, and frequently we were informed that one of the kids down the street had just lost their father. My mother consoled many of the military wives and their children, but she did not know from one day to the next if she still had a father for her own kids.

Not long after Dad left, a man showed up at our door. He said he had been sent by my dad to check on us and make sure we were all right. I remember the smell of his cologne, and I recognized him as one of Dad's closest friends. I was glad Dad was thinking of us enough to send someone. The man and Mom went to the living room to discuss important matters, while we kids went off to play. Later, when I came back in the house, I noticed the cologne smell again, and when I went into the living room, I was surprised that the man was still with my mom. My mom saw me and told me to go outside. The man turned around and started yelling at me to get out of the room. His voice was loud and he frightened me, so I ran out of there fast, but I knew that whatever they were doing was wrong. This was not my dad. Eventually the man left, and I was glad that he did not come around anymore.

The stress of military life during a war is more than anyone should have to endure. Mama and we kids anxiously awaited letters or any communication that our father was still alive. Most of the time, we received cassette tapes from him and could hear the guns and bombs going off in the background. Mama and Dad were not getting along, and they recorded their differences on the tapes back and forth to each other, prolonging the arguments. Mama's tapes back to Dad usually ended in tears.

At one point while we were still living in El Paso, my mom took a job at the local 7-Eleven store right down the street. It was good for her. It got her mind off the war and Dad. For a few hours at a time, she could concentrate on the store, instead of the constant pressure of the household chores, budget, and kids. It was good to see her getting out more, meeting people, and making new friends—like Maria, another lady who worked at the 7-Eleven.

When Mama worked, we had our share of babysitters, and boy did we have fun with them! We did not get along with most of them in Texas, because they were all Mexican, and we did not understand a word they said; likewise, they didn't understand us either! We did not make life easy on them. We were just normal siblings who fought with each other over the bathroom and the TV, but I am sure the babysitters did not appreciate our squabbles.

When summer approached and the temperature rose, we spent more and more time at the community pool. Mama decided we should learn to swim, so she signed us up for lessons. The day came when I was advanced enough to jump off the diving board. Mama made sure she was there for my debut. Right after I nailed the perfect dive and landed in the water, the boy in line behind me rushed in to show his dive. He did not wait for me to clear the area, but jumped and landed on top of me, leaving me disoriented under the water. Mama saw this and dove into the pool to save me. I thought I was drowning, and in my desperate attempt to climb up anything I could reach, I clawed my mother's bathing suit right off her body! It did not faze her a bit. Once she had me to safety and knew that I was all right, she simply put her suit back on as if nothing had happened.

After everything calmed down, the lifeguards approached her and proposed she become a lifeguard. She just laughed and told them it would not be the same, because this was one of her babies she had just rescued. Her quick reaction left a lot of people speechless that day—all the more because she was six months pregnant at the time.

Mama often invited groups of ladies from the base to the pool to play cards, and when she and Maria were scheduled for the late shift at the 7-Eleven, they frequently spent all day just sunbathing and talking poolside. On one of those nights, Mama had to work the late shift and Maria had left the store for the night. While Mama was closing up, a patron ran in and urged her to call the police, because someone had just been killed in the parking lot! Apparently, someone had gotten into an empty parked car and waited there in the back seat until the driver got in, and the criminal had slit her throat and robbed her. The victim turned out to be Mama's good friend, Maria.

Upon hearing the news, Mama was devastated, and she quit her job immediately. She became very depressed over losing her friend so violently. Because of that, coupled with many of the troops dying, she suffered through a tremendously difficult time. Three months after Maria's death, my mama went to the hospital to have the baby. When she came home, she surprised us with two babies! The twins, Debbie and Deon, were now added into the mix of our crazy household, and things got really exciting. There were six of us now—bottles and diapers were everywhere. We older sisters fed and became caretakers to our new sisters; it was like playing house, but we were doing it for real. My dad would not get to see the twins until they were three months old. Although I was young, I was very much aware that my mother was sad and lonely. I also sensed that she was apprehensive about him coming home.

Chapter 3
Dad's Return

I was seven years old when Dad returned from his second tour of the Vietnam War. I could tell Mama was happy and yet afraid at the same time. He seemed to have changed a lot. Even the look in his eye was different, and I did not feel close to him anymore. The night Dad arrived, he brought a shoe box full of pictures to the kitchen and emptied its contents onto the table. It was as if he were saying, "Here kids. Here is your surprise." There were hundreds of pictures of his tour in Vietnam. The pile covered the table. There were photographs of beheaded and charred corpses of Vietnamese prisoners and other atrocities. I suffered nightmares for years to come.

Looking back, I believe the military had a bizarre way of debriefing their troops after war. I wonder if what he suffered during two tours in Vietnam was part of the reason for what we kids endured. Even as young as I was, I knew what he'd done over there in the war had to have been horrible. I could also feel the pit of my gut telling me we were in for some rough waters ahead.

It upset me now just to watch him get ready for work in the mornings. He was much more reserved than he had been before, and we never really knew what he was thinking. No longer were we able to show him the affection and closeness we had once enjoyed. He just tolerated his children being around him. He seemed like a mad animal that would strike unpredictably. He just stayed quiet, with a strange look on his face, making it hard to feel safe around him any longer. There were no emotions or expressions about him.

It was impossible to know when he was happy, sad, or mad; he just kept the same look on his face all the time.

Most of the time, we just went quietly to our rooms when he was around. I do not recall helping with his boots in the mornings after he returned; instead, I hid from him whenever he came into the house. His voice and commands toward us were cold and almost scary. Soon he started accusing us of treating our mother horribly while he was gone, but we did not understand why he said that. We had not been any different and did not recall getting into enough trouble to warrant his daily lectures. I did not like him anymore and was scared of him. All of us kids scattered like roaches when he came into a room.

If anyone caused Mama any grief, it was our brother, Rick. He got into his share of boy problems, and my mother was always trying to fix whatever he got into. But even those little things were not serious enough for him to accuse us of treating our mother horribly.

Another displayed another example of his altered behavior when he noticed that the mixed vegetables in the pantry had been moved to the bottom shelf. My sister Terry and I had moved the cans weeks earlier, because we hated mixed vegetables. We thought that if she didn't see them, my mother would forget them and not serve them to us. When Dad asked who did it, we both admitted our guilt. The punishment consisted of him filling the cans with vinegar and handing them to us, with a spoon each. He said, "Here is what's going to happen. The last one finished will wear a diaper, and nothing more, outside to play for the day."

Mama was horrified but could not change his mind. Terry practically drank her can of vinegar and vegetables to keep from wearing the diaper. I was the unlucky loser of this race, and I remember how ashamed I felt. He even said, "I knew you would be the loser." No matter how hard I try, I do not remember how the clothes came off and the diaper on, or who did it. I do remember that when we got close to the back door, my hands dug into both the edges of the door, and I was hoping that he would not push me out into the fenced-in yard like an animal. I remember the push and jerk being horrible. I heard my shoulders pop while I was trying to hang onto the door. I walked around the yard, crying, while putting the palms of my hands onto my shoulders to try to relieve the pain. It did not work, but my hands did shield my uncovered body so that the kids could not see all. That was horrible pain, and it lasted what seemed an eternity.

I remember that event as if it were yesterday. Dad was being unusually witty and animated when yelling to the neighborhood kids to come around the yard to stare and mock me. I remember thinking that he was being just plain mean. I wished that he would go back to the war and never come home; I almost screamed it out at him. The constant rewind in my mind of how hopeless I felt stays with me to this day. I stayed backed into the corner of the yard and house, hoping to hide at least a little bit of my naked body. I backed my bottom against the hot house, so no one could see my backside as I tried to hide most of my front side. I was nine years of age, with nothing but a baby diaper on. I felt like an animal caged in the backyard for the kids and adults alike to laugh at and make fun of.

I looked to the adults to say something to help, but they knew Dad was a recent war hero, and he could do no wrong in their eyes, so they laughed with the kids. Humiliation and anger was consuming me, to keep my mind off what was happening. There had to be twenty kids and about ten adults who stopped by for the freak show in that fenced-in backyard that day. I was teased and harassed every day on the way to school for a very long time after that. I just got to the point where I chose not to hear and would duck around corners by myself as I walked to school. Older kids who had seen the event made sure they followed and mocked me on a regular basis.

Another time, we three older sisters found a book of matches. We were sitting there trying to figure out how to strike them when Dad came in. He came into the room and caught us. He made each one of us hold a match until it burned into our fingers, to teach us a lesson. I still have a white burn scar on my left index finger, where the fire burned deep into my finger. It was a very scary lesson, and I learned to fear him after that bizarre punishment. The fear was not only for me, but for my sisters, who were younger and much more afraid of our lesson. I can still hear us all screaming from the burning pain. He seemed amused by our punishment that day.

Dad also constantly pitted one of us against the other, making us compete in nasty ways. If there was a disagreement or an argument, he would put boxing gloves on us and make us literally fight it out. There were many occasions when we drew blood to appease him. My head bounced off walls countless times because I was not a fighter, and I held my punches, hoping that my opponent—my brother or sister—would get it over with quickly. We were taught to compete for everything, which did not make for very loving siblings. We three older girls soon learned not to trust each other.

One of my sisters quickly surmised that by getting perfect grades she could remain on Dad's good side. We would do anything to stay on his good side. Since we had changed schools several times in our moves to different bases, I had somehow missed the multiplication tables. When Dad realized that I did not know them, he made me sit in my bedroom for a whole summer learning them. I was not allowed to play with the other kids or go outside; I just had to sit in that miserable room writing out the tables for three whole months. He never helped me; he just tested me and browbeat me the whole way through. Rick would sneak into the room and use flash cards to help me. I guess it was survival of the fittest. Dad would use one sister's grades to scold the rest of us. "Why can't you be as good as she is?" Anything less than a B would get our butts beaten or grounded.

If it wasn't the buckle end of the belt, engraving D-A-V-E into our backsides, it was us having to take large bites of Dial bath soap and chew for up to an hour at a time. If we got sick, we started over. My stomach still retches when I smell that brand of soap. I remember too many times not being able to eat because of the welts in my mouth left by the soap's chemicals. Once I was at the end of the line for this punishment, and I was relieved to see the one next to me take the last bite. Dad simply went to the kitchen sink, grabbed a bottle of Joy dishwashing liquid, and said, "Open up." It was so awful. The only thing I could think of to keep myself from being sick was that I would never treat my own children like that, no matter what the offense.

What I did not know was that our nightmare had just begun. All the strange punishments began immediately after his return, and I believe life still might have been good if it had stopped there. What was happening between him and us was bad, but what I witnessed between him and my mother was unspeakable. Within the first week Dad was home, the fighting between Mama and Dad became awful. I knew something had gone wrong while Dad was away, because he was trying to make my mama confess to something that had happened between her and his friend, the one Dad had sent to check up on us. During their fights, Mama and Dad would throw things at each other as they yelled, and if I had not been so quick to duck, I am sure I would have been hit by one of their missiles. This sometimes went on for hours.

Mama would cry and Dad would be relentless, following her from room to room, yelling at her the whole time. Over the course of six months I watched my mother become more disconnected from the family. We older siblings were needed more and more by the twins. Rick never seemed to help much in that area, but Terry and I were getting really good at feeding, changing, holding, and rocking the younger ones. Mama was always sleeping or crying. She started withdrawing into her own world and becoming very distant. Her affection toward us became so strange. My dad was always mad that she would not, or could not, do anything. She became lifeless, with no expression.

One day, I found Mama in her bedroom packing her suitcase, with a look of sadness and fear at the same time. She was standing over her bed, sobbing; she told me she would be going away to attend her father's funeral. This was our Indian grandfather, whom we had never met. Weeks later, when she returned, she seemed to be a completely different person. She seemed unusually fragile. The day she came back I saw her reach into the hamper, pull out a bottle of pills she had been hiding, and slip a small handful into her mouth. She pressed her index finger against her lips, shushing me, and said, "Do not tell your father." Of course I promised her I would not, thinking I was protecting her.

Dad immediately started in on her. He followed her from room to room, and I followed the two of them around, like a shadow, watching her take more pills before Dad caught up with her in each room. She moved the bottle to different hiding places as she went, at one point putting it into her bathrobe pocket. Dad was yelling at her the whole time, and he was shouting, "Just admit it! Just say you did it!"

She was screaming, "Just do not give up the twins!" Then he turned to me and demanded I tell him where she was keeping the pills. As the oldest daughter, I had seen enough of his anger toward her, and I was not about to tell him anything. I did not understand what all the fighting was about.

What was he trying to get her to admit? And what did she mean about giving up the twins? I decided it was my turn to protect Mama. That night I slept with her, and Dad slept in my bed. When I heard the strange noises she was making while she breathed, I tried to wake her up, but I got no response. I did not realize that she was barely breathing. She was making horrible sounds in her sleep. The next morning, she was conscious just long enough to make me promise I would feed the kids and take them all out for a walk. Just as I left, I heard her tell Dad, "No matter what happens, promise me that you will not give up the twins." She was not making much sense to me, so I just did what she'd asked; I continued to gather my siblings and head out for our walk. We had not been out the door fifteen minutes when I saw an ambulance racing toward our house. Mama was taken to a hospital, where she stayed in treatment for severe depression for a whole month. I believe Dad wore her down so far that she felt she did not have a choice but to try to end her life. The part that was so hard about all of this was that he began to tell us kids that we had pushed her to this point! I blamed myself for everything that had happened to her.

Before this incident, I did not really know that pills could hurt anyone. I was only nine years old. The guilt was overwhelming, and what Dad said about it being our fault was starting to make sense and sink in. We were beginning to believe him. When Mama came home from the hospital, she was very quiet and did little around the house, always sleeping or just sitting on the couch without any emotion or expression. Dad cooked and became more of a drill sergeant than ever. Most of the time his orders were not very polite, and God help us if we had to be told to do something more than once. Between laundry and cleaning, our playtime came to an abrupt halt. Dad took Mama to the doctors several times a week. Most of the time, we sat in the waiting room while the two of them went into the office. Some of the doctors told us we needed to be good for our mother and make very little noise when we were home with her. We got to the point that we whispered most of the time and constantly tried to find quiet things for the twins to do so they would not upset her.

Dad was a Master Sergeant in the United States Army, and he was angry and embarrassed about my mother's illness, so not long after Mama came home, he arranged for us to be transferred to West Germany. This was because he knew we would be alone, with no family and no friends to have to explain to her out-of-control depression and the pills that would be sure to follow.

About a year after we transferred, Dad announced to Mama that her only sibling, Rita, had committed suicide. Rita had apparently taken her own life after she put her three children on the school bus one morning. Rita's four-year-old son had just been diagnosed with muscular dystrophy, and the doctor had told her that he would not live long. She could not cope with that news. Her husband knew something was wrong when she called him at work and asked him to come home to get their son off the school bus. He found her dead when he arrived. It happened nearly one year after their father had died. Dad did not tell Mama about this until Rita had been buried for about two weeks He took it upon himself to decide that she was too fragile to have gone stateside to the funeral. When he did finally tell her, I watched her crumble before him and slip into an even deeper depression, something that only I recognized from her earlier breakdown. Now that her mother, father, and only sibling in the world were gone, she felt so alone and abandoned.

At the young age of ten years, I found myself constantly assessing her for a breakdown of crying followed by a short period of pills, which usually meant a long time away from her children. Shortly after that, Dad left again for another extended assignment. I saw my mother start crying and not stop for three days. She went down behind our apartment building into the woods by a stream. I found her leaning against a tree, sobbing so hard she did not even know me. At this point, I was ten years old, and there were four younger sisters and my older brother to feed and take care of. I panicked, not knowing exactly what to do, because food was running low.

We had no idea how to contact Dad and were never told where the army had sent him. I begged Mama to tell me how to help, but she could not even answer me; she was so fragile and almost lifeless. Sometimes I had to put my face an inch away from hers so she knew I was there. No matter what I said or did, she would not respond. She completely stopped eating. I took sandwiches down to the woods, but she would not touch them. After a while, I began to feel dread when I walked away from her, because I was not certain that I would find her still breathing on my next trip back. I would walk away with hopelessness, remembering her smell and wondering if that would be the last time I walked away from her. My mother entered a depression that would be disastrous to us all. She was crying, not eating, drinking a lot of alcohol, and smoking more cigarettes than her small body could handle.

Shortly after this breakdown by the tree, she called the lady upstairs one day to take care of us for a little while, so she could rest. When the lady came, I began screaming, *"No! You can't take us! She will hurt herself—she will take the pills!"* I knew where Mama kept them, and I grabbed the lady's arm and dragged her into the next room to show her, but when I got there, they were gone. The lady carried me out, kicking and screaming because I knew what my mother was about to do. I knew she would take the pills, but no one listened to me, because I was only ten years old. An hour later Mama called, to our relief, and advised the neighbor that she felt better and was ready to have us back. We went back down to our apartment, but when we opened the door Mama was on the couch, unconscious, and so close to death that she had vomited and lost control of her bladder. The smell of urine and vomit was overwhelming, and to this day the smell stays with me. The flashbacks of the sight and smell are reruns no one ever wants to remember, but they never go away. It smelled like a stick of butter put into a pan and burned; it was awful!

The lady screamed over our commotion and tried to wake her by slapping and yelling at her. Her slack face did not make any expression; her eyes would not open or close; they were just frozen in a half-opened stare. At the age of ten, I felt so hopeless.

I continued to strike her lifeless face and scream for her to wake up. I continued until the squad arrived. When I looked around, I noticed Terry just standing there, stunned, and Sharon had gone into hysterical screaming. Rick was nowhere in sight, and the twins did not seem affected at all by what was going on. The neighbor grabbed Sharon and shook her until she became quiet; then she sat her on the floor against the wall. Terry just kept looking at me with a horrified expression. It made my stomach well up in my throat for Sharon and Terry, but there was nothing I could do but obey the lady by trying to wake our mother. It was all I wanted—for my mother to wake up.

My sisters were looking at me as if I were hurting her, and they seemed so frightened and confused. When the squad arrived, the paramedics began CPR. Mama survived, but she spent another month away from us. I cooked, did laundry, and played caregiver to the younger children once more.

We were soon transferred to another base in West Germany. Within six months, Mama took another overdose of pills and endured another stay in the hospital. By this point, Dad never stayed home anymore. He would do anything not to be at home. I really believe he was so angry at Mama for not having more control over her emotions that this was the point of no return for their marriage. We were in a strange country, and the people around us did not know us from the man on the moon. That is the way Dad wanted it; my mother had become too embarrassing for his military image.

When she came back home this time, she was seldom the same as the mom we had known years ago. There were brief moments when her witty humor would shine through, but they were fleeting. She was always in a placid state, never smiling or laughing as I remembered her. She slept more and more and disconnected from all of us to a point where she did not even know our names anymore. I found out that while she had been in the hospital they had administered electric-shock treatments. She never fully came back to us. She would have a good day once in a while, but those were very few and far between. I used to close my eyes and remember her smiling and think there was hope.

Christmas was fast approaching, and Mama seemed to want to give us a good holiday, but she rarely had the finances necessary. She often talked about decorating for Christmas, like our neighbors, but to actually go out and obtain the decorations was a daunting task. She relied on friends at the base for a ride and hoped that Dad would come home in time to buy all the presents. Most of the time, our family did not have a tree until the last minute. Mama smiled and laughed the most at Christmas time. We had an Advent calendar every December. Each day one of us opened a little door on the cardboard calendar to find a Bible verse written inside the tiny window. Mama would read the verse out loud; it seemed to touch her heart. We looked forward to hearing her read them, because she became so animated. Behind each door was also a chocolate candy, and we would take turns getting the candy until Christmas Day.

When Christmas Eve finally arrived that particular year, Mama danced around the windows and prayed that Dad would come home so we could all open presents. When she heard the van pull into the parking lot, she ran out, so happy to see him. When he finally opened the van door, he fell out drunk. He could barely walk into the house to open his gifts. The look on Mama's face, and the way her whole attitude changed instantly from a happy one to one of devastation, was so sad for me to witness. I did not even care if we had presents or not. The word panic did not come close to describing what I felt every time I saw that sad look in Mama's eyes. I knew what she was capable of when she became sad. My mother began to sink into an irreversible depression a little quicker each time.

When New Year's came around that year, it was a very special day for me. It was my birthday, and my mom had thrown a party. I was turning eleven years old—I had never had a birthday party before. She had invited my friends, planned games, and they had even brought presents for me! Mama was having so much fun; she was even playing all the kids' games. She was the happiest I could remember seeing her in a long time.

Three months later, Mama had another one of her good days. She was having lots of fun because the captain and his wife had come to our house to play cards. She seemed to be laughing and smiling more than I had seen in months. That night, when I went over to get my goodnight kiss from Mama, Dad motioned for me to go to bed. We had always exchanged hugs and kisses before bed, so I was disappointed to miss our nightly routine.

It was getting late, and I thought I had better not push my luck with Dad, so I hustled off to bed. It was just nice seeing her happy and being the life of the party. It had been amusing to watch from the shadows. At one in the morning I awoke to the sound of my sister, Terry, crying in the hallway. I opened my door to find her hugging the lady from upstairs. I asked what was going on, and she told me they had taken Mama back to the hospital. My sister said they had put a lot of tubes down her throat, and that she had lain naked on the living room floor while they pushed on her chest. In my sleepy state, I said she would be all right; she would be home soon. She always came back.

Dad finally arrived home from the hospital at seven in the morning. We were all awake and impatiently waiting to hear how she was. My dad's only words were, "Your mother will not be coming home. Your mother is dead." He turned and walked into the kitchen to fix a pot of coffee, as if he had not even said those words to us! I'm certain the crying and wailing that came from our house woke up the whole army base. My mother was dead at the young age of thirty-two years! During the next twelve hours (remember, I was only eleven), Dad ordered me to pick out my mother's favorite dress, shoes, and jewelry for her funeral. I remember feeling as if I had to put everything on before I gave them to Dad. I had to make sure they looked okay and even felt okay. At that age, I was about the same size as she was, and I spun in front of the mirror, watching the dress fly out in a twirling circle, just as she used to do when she wore it. I even had her pantyhose on. It just felt safe, as if she were still there with me. I pinned her favorite broach on the dress, just as she wore it. It was beautiful, but the sadness of having to give the clothes to Dad was overwhelming. It felt so final.

Terry, Sharon, Rick and Paula 1966

I became angry, because he was not even crying or showing any grief over losing her. While I was placing the broach on her dress, I overheard my father telling their friends that he would have her cremated, because that is what she wanted. This terrified me, and I asked, "Will we get to see her before you do it?" He promised me we would. Dad placed each of us kids with different families for the next two days. We never attended the service, nor were we able to see her again. We never even had a chance to grieve together those first horrible days. My last memory of my mother is watching her laugh while she was playing cards the night before.

Dottie sporting that military wife smile

I was so sad because Dad had not let me give Mama a kiss and hug goodnight, but I also remember taking notice of how happy she had been. On March eighth, two days after she died, Dad took us to the commissary to pick out new coats, shoes, and one outfit each. The three older girls matched, and the twins' outfits matched as well. The army flew all of us, along with Dad's best friend, home from West Germany to Columbus, Ohio, on a private 747 jet. It was the saddest, loneliest ride. We all cried most of the trip. Dad and his friend stayed drunk all the way home.

We landed at Port Columbus at noon. At the terminal, Grandma (Dad's mother) came running toward us, crying and out of control—but for Dad, not for our mother. She had never thought our mother was good enough for her son. I heard that several times over the next year. We arrived at our Grandma and Grandpa's house in the "Buckeye Addition" of Mount Vernon, Ohio, a few hours later. They had a very small two-bedroom home. We had stayed there for a couple of weeks before we'd left for Germany, so it was at least familiar.

Grandma's home always had the comforting scent of her peach dishwashing liquid. It made the whole house smell so good all the time. There was a backyard with lots of tall pine trees, and it was always fun to play around them. We were immediately packed into this house as tight as we could be. We would go to school at Elmwood Elementary School, just a short walk away. The kids in the neighborhood were really nice to us, walking us to school and showing us around.

Shortly after we settled in, a UPS package arrived. Dad called us all to the table and opened the box. He pulled out an urn, saying coldly, "This is your mother; now you have seen her," and then he put the urn back in the box. I was so confused about why he was handling the whole situation this way. I still wondered if she was really dead, because I never actually saw her body. I wanted to cry out and damn him for being so cold, but I knew that I would not live through it. I asked him if he would bury Mama, but I never got an answer; it was almost as if I didn't deserve one. He put the box up on a shelf in the closet in his room. It stayed there until we moved to the new house he bought us in the country.

When we were moving to the new house, an old family friend was walking around with the box that had Mama's urn in it. I watched her carry it and knew that she did not know what was in the box. I knew it was my mother's remains. I recall being very distressed, because up until now I had kept track of where this box was at all times since the moment it had arrived by courier at Grandma's house. This friend carried it for the longest time. When she finally found a minute to ask what to do with the box, Dad answered her with "Give me the box; that is Dottie's ashes." He then grabbed a green military shovel and went to the left side of the new house. I remember the shovel was folded in half, and he gave it a quick jolt to unfold it as he was going around the corner. When he came back, all he had in his hand was the shovel.

Chapter 4
A New Hell

Dad bought a nice house out in the country about four months after Mama died. It was small and only had three bedrooms, but soon he added three more in the basement for the five girls. The twins had the first room, at the foot of the stairs; Terry and Sharon shared the middle; and I had the third all to myself, clear to the back of the basement. They were very nice rooms. My Grandpa and Grandma's, Rick's, and Dad's bedrooms were upstairs.

We had been there for about two months, when one Sunday, Dad brought home our new stepmother, Lynn. She was a breathtaking contrast to my mother, who had not looked very good during the last couple of years of her life. Lynn was a flawless southern belle with perfect makeup, perfume, clothes, and the prettiest bright red hair. She walked in and introduced herself in an abrasive manner. As soon as I realized Lynn would be staying, I was saddened by the thought of my mother being replaced so quickly. I could not bear to watch my grandparents welcoming her, so I went down to my bedroom and started ironing my school clothes for the school week coming up.

The looks on my grandparent's faces were no happier than mine. They had just sold their home to move in and help Dad with all of us. I am sure they wondered at that moment what this meant for them. Within an hour of her arrival, Lynn decided it was time to come downstairs and meet us girls in our own space. Since my room was the last one in the basement, she went to the other girls first. I heard them run upstairs and the sliding door to the backyard close. I knew I was alone in the basement, and I had a bad feeling about this meeting. I heard over my head the footsteps of Grandpa and Grandma going into their bedroom and shutting the door, but then I heard Dad and Rick talking.

When Lynn entered my room, she asked me what I was doing, and I told her I was ironing my school clothes for the week. The mood I was in was not helping the conversation with her, and I kept thinking about my mother and how quickly our life was about to change. I stayed quiet and did not make conversation as quickly as she might have hoped. Since I was one of the gabbiest of the five sisters, this concerned even me. I just felt uneasy as she stood over me. Without a warning, she proceeded to rip the iron out of my hand, throw it down on the floor, and started beating me up! She grabbed at anything she could reach and started hitting me. Then she grabbed my hair and swung me like a rag doll. Within the first hour of her being in our house, I had a broken vein on my leg, several patches of missing hair, a bloody lip, fresh tears, and the shock of disbelief. She warned me not to say a word, or I would get it worse next time Within moments, she returned upstairs, with her little southern drawl, to meet the rest of the family—as if she had never done anything.

It got to where the beatings happened at least once a day, sometimes twice. She would threaten me with, "If you tell anyone, even your dad, you will get it twice as bad when he leaves; or worse, I will hurt the twins." She often did that anyway, because she knew my weaknesses were my feelings toward the twins and my feelings about my mother. Those two little girls were like my own children. My memory of them screaming on the other side of their bedroom door has haunted me all of these years.

Lynn beat Debbie one day for squeezing Prell shampoo into the bathtub while bathing. Within a couple of days, Debbie was admitted into the hospital. Lynn told the family it was a kidney infection, but after the beating Debbie had taken the day before, I always wondered. She would often beat my head against the wall until it bled, while making me repeat awful things about my mother that were not true. The beatings continued every day for the next year. Most of the time, when I thought she was done, she would wait about five minutes, then return and start all over again. I would just keep telling myself to hang in there, to not let her see me sweat for round one, and that she was guaranteed to return for round two.

The only time she would not hit us was if an adult happened to be upstairs, where he or she might overhear. That had not stopped her the first day she entered our home, due to the number of people upstairs. She must have thought they were all too busy visiting and chatting to hear anything. That day has never made any sense to me at all. From day one, I pegged her for the cruelest woman I had ever known.

Eventually, it got to the point where she did not even care if someone was upstairs. She would dare me to make a sound, saying, "Say one word, and I will be back to get you again, or even worse, I will get the twins." I ran away one night after a horrible beating. She had found a pair of scissors in the basement that I had forgotten to put away. She was furious and came into the bathroom while I was taking a shower. I was twelve at this time. She slid the shower door open, jerked me out, and proceeded to whip me with a thin leather belt from her dress before I even knew what was happening. I ran down to my room as fast as I could, covering myself with what clothes I could grab, while trying to get away from her.

I had to get out of there—she was getting more brutal every day. I wanted to tell Dad so badly, but I knew he would just say I was lying and punish me, so I ran away. Before I knew it, I was out the door and down the road. I came upon an old man and begged him for a ride to the sheriff's department. When I arrived, still with marks from the belt, I told the sheriff the whole nightmare with Lynn and what had been happening at our house. He put me in a holding cell of some kind to wait while he called our house. Soon, Lynn came to the station. She arrived dressed like something from the corner of the street; she was, of course, the prettiest thing the sheriff had ever laid eyes on. He turned to me and said, "If you ever run away from this lady again, you will spend a long time in here." Then he sent me home with her!

There is no way to describe the panic I was in, knowing Dad the way I knew him. My heart was beating a million miles a minute while I anticipated what would happen when she called Dad. I was so scared, not of being beaten again by her, but by how Dad would react. He would be so upset with me. When we got home, she called him, but her story was not even close to the truth, and she even added something like, "I am afraid for my life. Come home soon." I knew I was in for it this time. The welts that were left from the afternoon whipping from her belt were hurting so badly now; the pain throbbed to the beat of my heart as I agonized over what Dad would do to me when he got home.

I went to the cabinet and grabbed a large bottle of aspirin and a glass of water and went down to my bedroom, crying. I just wanted to escape the wrath of this evil woman, and I was so upset about the punishment I would receive from Dad. I would rather be dead than have to listen to the twins screaming as they endured Lynn's torture, and I would rather be dead than have to repeat things about my mother that were not true. Lynn would demand, after she banged my head against the wall, "Say it—your mother was a bitch, who just sat around and smoked her cigarettes and drank coffee! Just say it—she was just a lazy bitch!" For a while, she did this almost every morning before I went to school, mostly while I was trying to make lunches for the other kids. I mixed all the aspirin—one hundred pills or so— into the water and some sugar and drank it all. I went to the family room to find the twins watching a cartoon, hugged each of them, and walked back to my bed. All I could do was sob and pray that God would let me go. After a year of this torture, I just wanted to end it and go to sleep for good. I woke up the next morning feeling fine, as if I had never taken anything. I was so disappointed that the aspirin cocktail had not taken my life. I jumped up, expecting to at least be dizzy—but nothing. I went to school and hoped that no one would ask why I had bright red stripes all over my skin. No one did.

Looking back, I believe it was then that I acquired the ability to glare at people as if to say, "I dare you to talk to me—just leave me alone!" When I came home from school the next day, Dad was home, and I was quickly summoned upstairs to take my punishment. I could not tell him why I had run off to the police, because Lynn had already threatened me to keep me quiet. I said I did not know why I had done it. I remember him slamming me into the wall of the living room, but I can't recall anything after my head met the floor.

From the time Lynn moved in, most of our life was spent either outside or down in the basement in our own little sitting area by the washer and dryer. Those were the only places we were allowed, unless we were upstairs taking a shower, eating, or cleaning something. The adults lived in the upstairs, and we were not to be seen or heard unless we were called upon.

We were, however, expected to get all the chores done, and every day after school I became Lynn's personal "upstairs maid." I scrubbed and cleaned until I could not see straight. I would be so tired from school and cleaning that if there were a decent meal fixed, I was often too tired to eat; besides that, my stomach was so upset most of the time that it was hard to keep food down anyway.

After months of her abuse, I toughened up quite a bit; she could do whatever she wanted to me, but I just did not give her the satisfaction of seeing me cry. I had become an expert at hiding the pain. Then one day, out of the blue, I was surprised when Lynn said she wanted to reconcile and start our relationship over. As a peace offering, she told me she had a surprise for us girls, but we would have to wait until Saturday morning.

The day finally arrived, and she announced we were all going to the beauty shop. She was treating us to having our hair trimmed and styled. I could not wait! This was the first time in our lives we had been allowed to grow our hair out, and we all needed to have our hair shaped. When we got there, all three of us climbed up into the swivel chairs, eagerly anticipating our makeovers. We were imagining how they would wash and curl our hair, and we would feel like royalty.

But instead, to our horror, not a moment after we were in the chairs, Lynn barked her order to the stylists to cut our hair so short that we could not part it. After we had agonized through twenty minutes of hair-cutting, she came over to me to inspect the beautician's work. She ran her fingers through my hair and yelled, "Cut it shorter!" The women in the shop were aghast. Lynn was not very popular among the people in the salon at this point. There were at least twenty onlookers between all of the people waiting and the others getting makeup done.

After all these years, people still ask me if I was one of the little girls that endured the haircut that day; they still remember, too. I found a hooded sweatshirt to wear to school that day, but the kids were awful. For weeks, they would pull off my hood and make fun of me, killing any shred of self-esteem I had. While I hid it very well in school, the other kids knew there was something different about me. They treated me as though I were stuck-up or too good to talk to them, when in fact, I was just trying to hide the misery I was living through every day at home.

Not to my surprise, there were lots of kids living the same nightmares, and we always knew who we were. We just never talked about it; it was just the look we would share in passing. My objective was just to get through each day, one at a time. It was really unbearable; I feared for the twins' lives all the time. And I never knew what to do or say to keep from provoking some kind of punishment.

When school was finally out for the summer, things became a little more bearable. After we finished our chores, we could play like normal kids. Sometimes we went on all-day walks along the road and by the river, to get into town. We got to enjoy the majority of the summer while Dad worked and stayed at the base in Columbus. As usual, he would come home only when he needed to. That made for an even nastier stepmother dealing with the six of us, and now she brought her five-year-old to live with us. He was a sweet little towhead who was as confused as we were at the complete turnaround in his life. He had lost his father out of the blue.

There were not very many houses in our new neighborhood at this time, so we made paths in the wheat field next to our house and played house. One day, a pregnant cat, who looked as if she were going to have babies any day, appeared in the wheat field, so we brought her home and fed her. She was around for about three weeks when Dad finally noticed her. He went to the house, got his rifle, and called us all over. He pointed the gun at the cat and shot her right in front of us. Then he picked her up and threw her body over the cliff on the other end of our property. It was to teach us the "valuable" lesson of not taking in any strays. We all cried and felt horrible for the poor cat. My little sisters cried for hours. That is when I first learned about anger and resentment. I am not sure why, but this innocent animal really struck a chord with me when I watched him kill her.

When the other relatives came around to visit, it often made things even crazier. The worst part was overhearing my grandparents telling the aunts and uncles details of our stay in El Paso and Germany, with our mother's illness, as if we were not even in the room. Often the stories were so distorted that I had to go outside and hide behind the house, where I cried for hours, missing my mother. I hated to hear these people talking about her. It was so hard to hear their opinions about how they thought my mother was unfit. There always seemed to be a Dottie-bashing conversation whenever the family came over.

One day after the summer ended, Dad called us three girls upstairs. We could see Lynn in the kitchen, waiting for us, sporting a cat-that-ate-the-canary look. She seemed to be anticipating whatever was about to happen with great excitement. Something was very wrong. Dad had never called the three of us together without our brother. Rick was not even in the house, or anywhere around, which was even more alarming.

Dad started off with, "I want to congratulate you three girls—because of you, my son will be going back to live with his mother." Right away I was thinking, Rick is not really our brother? We had never been told that particular story. So far, we were a little confused, but it was not so bad. Dad continued to tell us that Rick had apparently convinced him that he, Rick, did not want another stepmom. Rick claimed that it was because of what my mother had done to him. He said the constant spankings he had received from her were all because of us three girls. He had told Dad that we three always got him in trouble with Mom and provoked spankings. Worst of all, Dad believed it! He then proceeded to administer our punishment by hitting each of us in the face with the entire force of his body behind it, bloodying us one at a time. His hand was not easy on any of us. At one point I saw one of my sisters run to get a paper towel to wipe away blood dripping down her chin from where her lip had been split. After my turn was over, and I tried to open my mouth, it made a snapping sound. To this day, I have to realign my jaw each morning to keep it from snapping every time I chew or open my mouth.

Sharon

Terry

Rick

Rick's story: *My name is Dave Richard Jr. I am the brother in the family, and here is how this nightmare of a mess began. I was asked to share what I remembered of this very brief, but devastating, time for all of us. We had been close siblings up until now. It is now July of 2008, and I am, for the first time, revealing this knowledge to help you, the reader, understand the beginning of this very unthinkable nightmare.*

It was a Friday and I was fourteen years old. The bus doors slid open, and I was glad that I had left Mount Vernon school system behind me for a couple of days. (At least the people in Ansbaugh, Germany—where we were stationed in the U.S. Army before we lived in Mount Vernon, Ohio—seemed real and not so shady and backstabbing.) As I entered the house and was going down the hallway, the bathroom door opened, and a ring-covered hand latched on to my vest and pulled me inside! It was Grandma Teresa. She pulled me past her, locked the door, and sat on the side of the tub. Grandma T was not the smallest grandma, and I remember thinking as she was sitting there that those black stretch pants were really being tested.

Now, Grandma normally was very upbeat, with lots of smiles, shining eyes, a Marlboro cigarette in one hand, and a cup of Folgers in the other. But today was very different. She was wringing her hands together. There was a cracking in her voice, and her eyes were red and moist. Something was wrong, and I could feel myself getting uncomfortable and scared! What Grandma revealed to me next would change my life and the lives of Paula, Terry, and Sharon. She told me, "Monday morning, you are being sent to military school until the age of twenty-one, and the three older girls are being sent to three different foster homes!" I guess she did not really know how to be easy about it, so she just said it.

"So, you have two choices, Rick: wait till Monday and go be a little soldier boy, or give your mom a call." She handed me the phone number, unlocked the door, peeked out of the bathroom door, and left. I suddenly felt as I had the first time I smoked a cigarette in Ansbaugh. I could not see straight. My knees felt weak, and I had a sickening feeling in my gut. I had the phone number in my hand, and I was staring at the phone, wondering how I was going to pull this off. What was I going to do?

Up until a few years ago I had thought my mom was dead. Dad had lied to me and told me she was, to keep me from wanting to return to her. I discovered through some incoming mail that it was a lie. I had not seen my brother or sister, who remained with my mom, since I was much younger. What about Paula, Terry, and Sharon? As I picked up the phone, I remember thinking that the lousy school lunch and I were going to get reacquainted. The conversation with Mom was quick and to the point. "Come and get me." I hung up the phone.

When Mom and her husband, Johnnie, arrived, chaos ensued. The next several hours seemed like an eternity, I was shaking so badly. I had no control over what was about to happen to me. The parents were hashing things out, grandparents were trying to get out of the way and hidden, and Paula, Terry, and Sharon had, as far as I knew, had no clue. But in the end, I got to walk out of there with my mom, never to look back again. I was sad about leaving my sisters (I actually had just found out they really were not my full sisters), but I was so relieved to be out of there forever.

Sharon, Paula, Terry & Rick 1st group visit since 1994

We three girls tried to take in the reality of what had just happened, but Dad made us stand still, saying he was not finished. He told us, "I am not your father; I only adopted you three girls when I married your mother. Your birth name is Krohmer." He went on to say that he had adopted the three of us in 1964. Rick was his child from a previous marriage. Our ages at the time of adoption were one, two, and three, and he told us that our real father was a drunk and a gambler who lived somewhere in Georgia.

He said he had contacted our birth father, Mr. Krohmer, but he did not want us. He said Mr. Krohmer had let us girls and our mother almost starve to death before Dad—or should I say—*Dave* "rescued" us. We stood in total shock from both the physical blows and the news that we not only didn't have a mother, but now we didn't have a father. We were officially orphans.

His next announcement would change the rest of our lives. He said, "When you arrive home from school tomorrow, there will be three people here waiting to take you to foster homes, and you will not be allowed to talk or visit each other for any reason. You will not see the twins again." Then he warned us to watch our backs because someone would always be watching us. I started thinking we really might have killed our mother, because only criminals would be treated like this! By now we had heard that phrase, "you girls killed your mother" so often that I was starting to believe it.

Never mind unspeakable, now our lives were on the edge of unthinkable! The whole world stopped and then started spinning out of control all at the same time. My sisters were crying so hard that buckets would not have contained their tears. Sister Terry was rocking back and forth as if she were ready to fall, and sister Sharon was crying with no expression on her face, as if the word *hopeless* had hope compared to what was before us. I can hardly put into words what was going through my mind as I stood there watching the other two.

I had four sisters that I would watch being torn apart. I felt completely abandoned, and there was no one there to help. I thought back on the night I had heard my mother say, "Just promise you won't give up the twins," and I knew that she had foreseen this day happening. As I watched this all taking place, I went inside my mind, with a million questions and a dreadful sadness. I felt as if we were going to a concentration camp, or worse. We were middle-class military children who had never heard the term *foster home*, and we had no idea what this was. Everything I had heard during that dreadful fight between Mama and Dad that night all fit together; I finally understood it all.

Something changed in me that night, and it changed me down to the raw soul of my being. The sadness our mother had experienced up until the day she died was all about her knowing we would have to live this moment. She knew Dave well enough to understand that her little girls would never get the chance to grow up together, and I believe this made her the sad woman she became in the end. The many times my mother said she had something to tell us—and then could not completely express her thoughts—made sense now. She would break down and cry with a sadness no one could ever comfort. This was what it was all about. She had wanted to warn us about Dave and his plan.

Now Dave was finished with us and excused us to go back to our bedrooms. The other two girls quickly went downstairs, but I wanted to see what he would do next. Still totally unable to move, with my face and jaw throbbing, I watched him call our grandmother—or should I now say "adoptive grandmother"? I heard him tell her that it was over. His words were so creepy. It was as if the whole family had been waiting to hear that he had finally told us the truth. He said to her, "The other two girls cried, but Paula did not. She will be the one who ends up in a padded cell or jail." Those words still ring in my head today. As devastated as I was, the words that came into my mind were, *We will see about that.*

Chapter 5
The Journey to New Homes

At twelve years old, and right after being separated from my family, I was in the car and at the mercy of my caseworker. We were heading for the Knox County Children's Services Center. A lady named Judith Goodhand introduced herself as the director and extended her hands to me in a welcoming gesture. She impressed me as one person who truly cared. She was very petite and dressed professionally in a skirt suit. She had strawberry-red hair, cut in a very short, sophisticated style. She had kind eyes and a knowing smile, and her small, round face was covered with freckles. At the time, in a world full of uncertainty, knowing someone who had anything in common with me was a comfort—between the two of us we had a lot of freckles. I liked the perfume she wore; it was very crisp and clean. Her eyes were lined with bold eyeliner, and she looked right into mine when she spoke to me, making me feel calm.

The Wall – Paula's Foster Care File Picture 1974

I did not know just yet what role she would play in my life, but I sensed she had powers that most could not match. When she spoke, I listened, even though I cannot quite put into words why I felt that way. She seemed to peer directly into my soul, knowing what was happening in my heart before I even had a chance to tell her. I was still in shock from the rejection of my "parents," while the caseworkers continued to put my file together. After fingerprinting me and taking photos, they officially declared me a foster child. I did not even know what that meant, but I remember just wanting to die. How could this all be happening?

When I was done meeting with Judith and being processed, she sent the caseworker back over to me, and we were off. We drove for about thirty minutes to a small town called Amity, Ohio, and we pulled into the driveway of a quiet and nicely kept farm. The caseworker did not tell me anything about this family except the parents' first names, Mary and Brian. It was suppertime when we arrived. She carried in the little grocery sack of belongings Dave had given me and dropped it on the floor, as we walked toward a large kitchen table. She introduced me to the group seated at the table, and the she left. Her job was over. Sitting before me were Mary and Brian, their birth daughter, and three foster sons. The meal consisted of spaghetti and meatballs, which was in a large kettle in the middle of the table. I stood watching them eat until someone invited me to sit down and eat with them.

After supper, their daughter, Cammie, showed me where I would sleep. My bed was in the same room with her, and she was very nice. I eventually became very close with this new sister, but she did not compare to my own. Mary and Brian owned a bar in Mount Vernon, so I seldom saw them. We foster kids ran the house while they were working. Since they worked nights, many times they came downstairs in the afternoon, hungover, asking what time of the day it was. Many mornings we had to go into the bar to help them clean up after a big crowd. It was not always bad and scary there. We did have some good times on the farm; they had a horse that I sometimes rode with my new sister.

In the beginning, a benefit was that I still attended the same school as my sisters. I could sneak to their lockers to arrange meeting places for us. My sisters and I had to meet in secrecy, because our foster parents told me not to make any contact with my sisters in school. The hall monitors and teachers had been instructed to keep us away from each other. There were times we met in the boiler room in the basement of the school, and sometimes we met in the bathrooms. The middle school janitor must have heard conversations about us not being allowed to talk to each other, but he would arrange for us to see each other in his office occasionally, when he could get away with it. He was a kind old man. This is where we found out we were each okay in our different homes. We also talked about the twins and what they must still be going through. During these secret meetings, we would brainstorm to try to figure out what we had done so wrong to have caused our separation.

After I talked to the caseworkers about my new foster parents, who were always hungover or not at home, they investigated my accusations, and the other foster kids and I were removed. The day

I left, Mary threatened that when I became twenty-one she would look for me and "kick my ass" for ratting them out to Children's Services. After what Lynn had done to me, this little woman did not scare me with her threats; she just disappointed me. I can only guess that the money they were making through the foster program paid a lot of their bills—though it never helped any of us out. That home lasted from October until April.

My next foster home was with a young couple, the Kellies, who had not been married very long. They were wonderful people and included me into their nightly biking trips. The first day they bought me a three-speed bike, and we rode every evening all over the back roads of Mount Vernon. More than anything, I remember their fighting. While being with the Kellies was tolerable, it did not last long, because Mr. Kellie was transferred to Texas with his company. I chose not to go with them, because my chances of reuniting with my sisters would be almost impossible. A caseworker soon came with a box to pack up my things for the next home.

Next I moved in with the Swansons, which was truly a strange household. It was filled with mixed signals from the first day, so I knew this one wasn't going to last. They had a six-year-old little girl who was very sweet, and Mr. Swanson was kind of shy and never said very much. Mrs. Swanson, however, was always upset about something. She would confront me with things like the electric bill being too high from me taking long showers. I never knew how to act there. The only nice memory I have from there is that at Easter they bought me a necklace with a *P* engraved on it. I still have that today. One day I was down at the neighbor's house playing, and the kids told me they had heard I was moving out, because my new mom was pregnant. The whole neighborhood knew before I did that there would be another move! I ran down to the Swansons to see if the rumors were true. Mrs. Swanson acted as if the neighbors telling me did not even matter! She just said that she could not have a teenager around while she was pregnant, because it was too nerve-wracking for her. Two months after I had moved in, I was moving out. I heard later that she had her baby stillborn. I cried for them, no matter how hurt I was about having to move again.

Next I was moved into the Clark family, with two small children, ages eight and nine. When I arrived, the foster mom was in the hospital, having undergone a hysterectomy. Around three in the afternoon, an hour after I had been dropped off, Mr. Clark called, and I agreed to send the hired sitter home and babysit, since something had come up and he could not get home as soon as planned. I showed myself around the house and made the kid's supper in my strange new surroundings. The children showed me the room their mother had prepared for me, and I got them fed, bathed, and all of us down for bed that night. Around midnight I heard loud voices downstairs, when Mr. Clark came in with his friend, drunk. I heard words I had never heard before and heard stumbling over the furniture downstairs. I was so scared I would not get up and walk down to meet him. The next morning, I fixed the little ones their breakfast while my new foster dad slept in until eleven. When he finally got up, I was very angry and upset, but I forced myself to meet him. We both knew his behavior was wrong. After that, he tried hard to make up for what he had done, but I never did trust him at all. I never told the caseworkers about this. Mrs. Clark came home from the hospital about three days later. She was so nice and always in a good mood. Even though she was delightful to be around, I knew this home was not going to last, either. Mr. Clark had just learned that his plant was closing down and he, too, would soon be transferred to Texas. Over the next five months there were many good times, though. I grew very close to my new foster mom. She even let me have a black cat, which was awesome, because I needed that cat. Often he climbed the tree by my bedroom window to get in and sleep with me at night.

The Clarks allowed me to visit the neighbor's farm. I would go every few days to brush their two horses. One day I looked up to notice a boy sitting on the fence watching me. He began asking me questions and talked to me as if he had known me my whole life. He was fifteen and I was thirteen. Jack was very sweet, never questioning what I was going through. He knew something was not right about me but was not quite sure what it was. Sometimes we would just talk for hours. Jack was the first friend that I confided in about what had happened to my sisters and me. Eventually we began walking home from school every day. He did no more to me than hold my hand, and we became best friends.

Mrs. Clark did not approve of this relationship, because she did not think I should have a boyfriend at my age. She became cross with me all the time after that, but of course, the angrier she became the more I wanted to see him. Soon the Clarks transferred to Texas. A caseworker came to the house with a box, and away I went again.

This time I ended up at the home of Mrs. Williams. This home was different from the others in that it was only an emergency, temporary foster home. This was a new concept, and I was told it could last anywhere from one to six weeks. But what Children Services did not know about Mrs. Williams was that even though she knew each foster child who came into her home would leave soon, she was very angry about it. Over the next two weeks she complained that all the kids who came through her home used her. She was very hard on me, so things were always tense. She lived on a horse farm outside of Mount Vernon. She felt ladies should act like ladies all the time. She even smacked my hand when I dipped my toast into an egg before taking a bite!

Mrs. Williams had three grown daughters, and I passed a lot of time with them and their husbands, helping clean deer pelts during hunting season. Other family members were really nice to me also, and when I think back, I realize maybe they knew I needed to be rescued from her. Two weeks with her seemed like a year. Thank God I had been taught how to make my bed, because she was a tough one. In spite of all the bad stuff that had happened in our original home, we had been taught table manners and how to set a table properly. Thank goodness, because this little woman was very much a proper lady and expected the same out of me. Mrs. Williams was very particular about everything.

Chapter 6
God-Sent

After the move to Mrs. Williams', I acquired a new caseworker, Buffy Fisher. She was one of the greatest people I had the privilege of meeting and becoming friends with. It was not long into our counseling when she told me, "No matter what, do not ever let these experiences change your personality—never get hard." Buffy was aware that I had been through six foster homes by this time, and she was determined to help me.

One day she shared a great new idea, which was to arrange a meeting with any prospective foster parents and to treat this meeting like a job interview. We would meet them over supper at their house and discuss the option of me living there. They would be able to see who I was and make conversation with me, and I would be able to listen to them and get a chance to look around their home. I would even be told ahead of time where their house was located. This was a much different approach than before, when I had just been deposited at strangers' houses.

The new parents' names were Larry and Bonnie Ulrey. The dinner interview went great, and toward the end of our interview, Mr. Ulrey asked if I wanted to live with them. He said he really wanted me to be a part of his family. It felt really good to be asked personally and to have some say in the matter. For the first time, I had some control in my own life. I told him I had a black cat and would really like to bring him with me. He said that was fine, and we agreed I would move in that very weekend. I was truly happy for the first time. Both Larry and Bonnie told me they looked forward to me being a part of their family and could not wait till I came back. In fact, I did not even want to leave; I wanted to stay that night. I already felt such a peacefulness in their home.

Saturday morning came, and Buffy picked me up for my move to the Ulreys'. Mrs. Williams, my short-term foster mother, was very emotional but understood that I would be better off where I was going. I assured her I would stay in touch, and I did, until she died about fourteen years later from cancer. She was a very caring and loving woman who just did not know how to disconnect from her temporary foster children. It was difficult for her each time one of us left. I arrived at the Ulreys' around nine in the morning. Bonnie showed me to my room and told me she had a big day planned for us to go shopping. When I saw my room, it was sterile and all white, with no bedspread, curtains, or anything in the room but the bed and dresser.

I looked at her and asked if this was really my room, and her response was, "Paula, this is your room. When we go shopping today, you will pick out the color you want your room, your bed cover, sheets, pillows, and anything you need to make this room comfortable. This is your room now." I was suddenly feeling a little light-headed and a little surer that they wanted me to be a final part of their family. They were giving me choices that most birth children would receive, choices to decorate my own space. What a feeling! I will never forget it. I do not remember all the places we went, but I do remember all the bags of clothes and frilly girl stuff she let me choose. We shopped half of the day just to decorate my new bedroom, and it was so much fun!

Bonnie 1975 – always a smile and happy thought

The smiles during this shopping experience were happy and yet sad. Tears would creep into the moment as I fought them back. I kept wishing that both Terry and Sharon were with me and that they, too, would be coming to live with the Ulreys. I had outgrown the only clothes I had, that one bagful that had traveled with me to the foster homes that year. When we arrived back home, I sat in the middle of the living room floor just staring at all the bags in front of me, in total disbelief. I hoped that wherever my sisters were, they had everything they needed, too.

For the first time, I felt good about where I was and the people who made up my new family. This was finally my new home and family. In my mind I wondered if finally I had made it through the gauntlet. There were no other siblings living with us. Sometimes I really loved it, but often it was uncomfortable. I wasn't used to being the only child. All the attention was on me.

My new foster sister, Linda, was twenty-three. She no longer lived with her parents, but she came almost daily to visit. There were two horses on the farm that we often rode together. She was very close with her parents, and she and I also became close. Linda had one of the most unusual, witty personalities and was very comfortable to be around. Her wit reminded me of my own mother's. Linda was always full of one-liners that were meant to make her audience laugh and feel at ease. She was ornery and sassy and became my horse-riding friend for years. I respected her and cherished our new friendship.

During the first week of my stay at the Ulreys' home, Bonnie told me I needed to forgive everyone in my past who had ever hurt me or my sisters. She explained that if I couldn't do this, I would never be able to love anyone in the future, including any children I would have of my own. This was really a profound, intimate conversation that touched my heart and made me think long and hard about my past. She also said it was most important that I love myself. Looking back, I see that I must have really been a mess, because she could see that my emotions were out of control. I did not know if I loved anyone, including myself.

Bonnie said it was vital to my survival to understand this before I turned eighteen, because after that I wouldn't have the right to blame anyone else for my actions. I would be completely responsible for my actions from that day forward. That was why I needed to work on forgiving everyone from my past. I took it very seriously. This was a conversation I would replay in my mind repeatedly for years to come. She truly touched my heart that day. At the end of our conversation, Bonnie asked permission to pray for me. I wasn't sure about it, but I said okay. She scooted a little closer to me, wrapped her arms around me, and prayed out loud. At that moment I wondered if this was what real mothers did for their children. Was this something we had all missed?

One of the first tests of my new attitude came one Saturday morning when Bonnie took me grocery shopping. We were walking through the store, but were not together at that moment, and I saw Aunt Jane, Dave's sister, doing her own shopping. I had not seen anyone from the family since I'd lived with Dave, so I was very excited to see her and ran up to her to say hello. She held her hand out and stopped me before I could get too close. She blurted out in front of many strangers that she didn't know me and told me never to talk to her. She insisted that I had ceased to exist for her. Then she turned around and walked away as if I were some kind of leper. I don't remember anything stinging quite like that moment. Of course, I did not mention it to Bonnie, and she did not know why I was so sad and quiet all the way home.

As normal as I seemed to Bonnie and Larry in the beginning, I know that they soon found out they had their hands full with me. Even I did not understand how messed up I was emotionally— but what I did know was that if all of us sisters could be together again it would make us feel better. At this time in the '70s, a foster parent did not have the right to know the complete backgrounds of the children they took in. Under some ridiculous law, the state protected the parents who gave them up.

It was so strange that we three sisters were not even allowed to know why our dad gave us up. I would endlessly ask but would always be told we were better off not knowing what he had said. The caseworkers would say, "Just move forward, and go on with your life." It was a big secret, which we would never officially be told. How could they tell us? The caseworkers were not even allowed to know where we had actually come from or why we had been separated.

My new parents did know they had a thirteen-year-old girl who was pretty frantic to make connections with her sisters. Knowing that this was affecting me so much, Larry and Bonnie supported my every effort to find them. After much persistence on Bonnie's part, she was able to convince the caseworkers that we needed to at least visit with each other—so we began scheduled visitations!

As much as we missed each other, during these visits we would fall into the old habits of competitiveness that Dave had instilled in us. After each visit we would be angry and uncommunicative and get into trouble at our respective foster homes. The foster parents and caseworkers began shortening the visits—instead of getting us family counseling.

Whenever any of us made contact with the twins, via phone or an occasional quick visit arranged by Grandma, we were even more miserable, because we discovered that our stepmother was beating them worse than ever. After a while, we could not keep tabs on them because Dave moved them to Michigan. Dave and Lynn returned the birthday and Christmas presents we sent, not allowing contact of any kind.

Since none of us was able to do anything for them, this left me very angry inside. Yet Bonnie and Larry were very understanding.

They truly wanted us girls to be together again. In fact, they wanted the three of us to live together with them.

I came home from school one day to find dozens of people in the house, fixing food and laughing. I was not sure what was going on and why all the festivity, but I assumed it was a luncheon for church women, which Bonnie frequently hosted. Suddenly, though, my sister Sharon jumped out of a closet and announced she had moved in! Everyone chimed in and started clapping and crying as I started crying. Bonnie and Larry stood each with one arm around the other, watching the whole scene. I was crying and jumping, and Sharon was blowing some noisy horn and jumping up and down with glee. Everyone was happy for us. The looks on their faces will never leave my mind. This was the best gift I had ever been given. Now I actually had one of my sisters with me as part of our new family!

But it was strange that even though this is what I had been praying for, and I was excited, Sharon and I did not even hug. We had no idea how to accept this kind gesture. I had written my sisters off as dead, and I think that I had even grieved their loss. They must have done the same, since now neither Sharon or I knew how to reconnect. None of the adults was prepared for the trying times that we would have to go through.

The Ulreys' own children, three grown sons and a grown daughter, treated us as if we had been a part of the family all of our lives. And as much as we wanted that acceptance, we did not quite know how to feel and accept it. We were uncomfortable with even the nicest things that were done for us, because we were not used to it. I was cautious and fearful of rejection every day. The threat of caseworkers coming with boxes to pack at a moment's notice hung in the shadows. If I learned to care back, it might all end tomorrow.

This fear would haunt me in relationships for many years to come. For the entire first year I lived with the Ulreys, I came off the school bus looking for strange cars and anticipating that someone would be there to take me to a new home. I could not share those fears with anyone. I remember the first time I began to feel this living arrangement might be permanent, when Larry introduced me to a group of his friends as "daughter number two." I never heard the words "foster daughter" from either of my new parents. I even hid these positive feelings from them.

Bonnie woke up each morning at five and immediately headed for the corner in the living room she designated for her daily devotions. She wrote out her prayers for each one of her daughters; she even included our younger sisters, Debbie and Deon. We still did not know where they were, but Bonnie kept them in the prayer notebooks with our names inscribed on them. This was one of the many ways Bonnie had managed to gently chip away at the walls I had erected to close people out. It did not happen overnight, but took several years. She was even able to induce me to feel comfortable enough to let her ask questions about what had happened in our past. I always knew that if I screwed up she and Larry would love me anyway, and it was that unconditional love I experienced in their home that made me so grateful.

Chapter 7
Troubled Teenager

Paula 1976 at Larry and Bonnie's

Jack, the boy I had met while living at the Clark's, was the only close friend I had known before moving in with Bonnie and Larry. The Clark's home had been my fifth foster home, and by now I had known Jack for almost a year. He had been there for me emotionally through my past three homes. I could always talk to him and tell him about my fears and frustrations with all of my new families, as well as my feelings of rejection and inadequacy. He was soft, kind, and quiet, and up until now, no one had been able to get into my mind and heart as he did—or so I thought.

Shortly after I moved in with the Ulreys, Jack started pressuring me to sleep with him. I was only fourteen, and he was fifteen, but he threatened that he would quit seeing me if I did not. At that point in my life, I was unwilling to risk losing his companionship. The scary part was that I did not truly know what "sleeping with him" really meant. I just knew that if I did not give in to whatever it was he wanted something else bad would happen, and I would lose my tenuous sense of security.

I frequently babysat for a family, and the next time I babysat I invited Jack to come watch television with me after the little boy was asleep. Once he got there, he gave me the familiar ultimatum once again. I was so afraid to lose him that I gave in. I had no idea what it was I was about to do, but I went through with it anyway. I was scared because of everything that had happened to me up till this moment, and now sex was more or less being forced on me.

I remember I kept using the little guy I was babysitting as a stall and kept checking on him. The last time I checked, I just kept pacing, wanting to change my mind, but not even sure what it was I did not want to do. When I walked out into the living room, Jack pulled me down on the floor and took my pants off, leaving my shirt on. The whole thing was fast and there was no tenderness. He was done within minutes. Afterward, I felt ashamed.

I remember running to the bathroom to throw up. I was crying. It was truly one of the most horrible experiences of my life. I do not think he was even aware or even cared that it was my first time. By the time I was dressed and back into the living room, he was gone. He did not even say good-bye. Three months later, I found out I was pregnant. My sister Sharon had only been moved in for six months by now and she was very angry knowing that I would be leaving and her behind. I went to Bonnie and told her that something was not right, that I was not having periods for the last few months. She asked me if I had had sex with Jack, and I told her that I thought I did once. She was very angry and unhappy.

She immediately planned an appointment with the doctor. I was fourteen years old and ten weeks pregnant. The baby was due on January thirtieth, which would have made me just barely fifteen. Bonnie had to let Children's Services know, so she called Judith Goodhand and gave her the news. Immediately I was counseled about the choices I had and told that I did not have long to make the decision.

Larry and Bonnie were completely removed from the situation. Judith told them she would help me make the decision that was right for me, and then she would let Larry and Bonnie know what my decision was. I tried to convince everyone that Jack really loved me and he would not let our baby be aborted, and finally I won a chance for him to meet Judith and prove his love. Judith drove me to find him at the community swimming pool. As I approached, he was walking up to the high dive. I stopped him and told him I wanted him to come with me to explain to Judith that he loved me and that he wouldn't let them kill our baby. I'm sure he was shocked; after all, this was the first time he'd heard I was pregnant. He looked at me and said, "I do not know what you are talking about. I do not even know you, and I have never touched you before in my life." Then he turned and walked away! My heart died.

Judith sat in her car watching the whole ordeal. This was exactly what she had tried to tell me would happen. But I had really believed, beyond a shadow of a doubt, that he would protect me. The betrayal by this boy who had told me he loved me for a whole year, and then walked away, made me feel the painful rejection I had feared for so long. This was the same rejection I had planned to avoid by sleeping with him—whatever that meant. Over the next two weeks, my caseworkers counseled me about what decisions I could make. They gently went over the fact that I was not the same as any other teenager; I belonged to the state of Ohio, as a ward of the state, and I was governed by a whole different set of rules. I turned my head and pretended not to hear or understand what they were saying. I had it in my mind that I simply was not going to have an abortion, but they had it in their minds that I was.

Judith also knew that Larry and Bonnie, who were my main source of support, were opposed to abortion on moral grounds, so she herself took the responsibility of driving me to the clinic.

She stayed as close to me as the medical staff would permit. I can remember as if it were yesterday the breakfast with Bonnie before Judith picked me up. She was so upset, for reasons I did not understand at that young age. She prayed for me, with her arms wrapped tight around me, before Judith picked me up for this uncertain journey I was about to take.

The nurse in the clinic gave me sedatives to calm me and repeated several times that it would not hurt and that what was in my belly was not a baby; it was just a fetus. I was sick and scared. I was also the youngest girl in the clinic. The next youngest out of twelve other women was twenty-six years old. There are no words to explain the nightmare that occurred that day. I can, however, explain the rocky feeling of just wanting to throw up every minute from the first step into the door. The procedure they used was a suction abortion, and the pregnancy was terminated at twelve weeks. I can still close my eyes and see and feel every second of that procedure. It is like a film that just replays over and over in my head.

While Larry and Bonnie never accepted my choice, they were there to support me. About four months later, in one of my classrooms, I found a bulletin board adorned with a string of posters. They depicted stages of human development from conception through birth. Curious to see the twelfth week, I followed the board in slow motion—and I felt as if something had stabbed my heart. I had never felt so deceived and lied to in my life. I was looking at a baby with a perfectly formed body, fingers, toes, eyes, etc. It was at this moment that the word "murderer" sank into my heart like an anchor thrown from a ship into the ocean. And this anchor was trying to drown me along with it.

The room started to spin, and even though I knew my classmates were talking because I could see their mouths moving, I could not hear a thing. I walked out of that classroom and down the hall; I was sweating heavily. I left the school and ran toward town, crying and ducking behind trees to throw up several times along the way. Finally, I sat down to catch my breath and waited for the tears to clear my eyes, before I called Bonnie to come and get me.

When she came, I climbed into the van and blurted out what I had seen. She looked for a quiet place and parked the van beside a shade tree. She came into the back seat, grabbed me, and just rocked me. She assured me she did not agree with the decision and that if she had had her way things would not have happened the way they did. This was the first time I saw Bonnie cry. She kept saying, over and over, "This should not have happened. We should not have let them do this to you."

After this experience, my self-confidence was so far gone that I walked around for months with my head down, not ever looking up at people. I was so ashamed of what had happened. Larry knew this and tried to make things better. He would tell me often that I was smart and pretty, and he would say to me, "You can do anything you want to do and be anything you want to be." I was not used to that. I had a really hard time accepting his compliments. In fact, the first time he said something nice to me, it felt as if he had hit me. Dave had used to pick me out of the crowd as being the stupid one. He would tell people that I was the only kid that would try to put a square peg into a round hole. He really destroyed my self-esteem.

I just wanted to stay hidden away from everyone. When my new parents would say something nice, I would cry miserably. It took many years to realize that Bonnie and Larry meant what they said, and it took many more years to convince me that I was not stupid, ugly, or just plain worthless. Worse, after being told by Dave and Lynn that we girls had murdered our mother—now I could honestly say that I was a murderer with this abortion. It was many years before I realized that the decision to abort this baby had not been mine.

I remember one Sunday we had just arrived home from church and I had stepped out of the van, when Larry looked at me and said, "Bubbles, you sure are a pretty girl." I was so taken aback by this statement; I almost crawled back into the van and hid! *Bubbles* was the nickname he gave me the first night I came to their house. Both Bonnie and Larry always had a way of making me feel special. We all grew closer over the years. I could never call either of them Mom or Dad. Calling them by their names was more special to me, since the words *Mom* and *Dad* in my world usually meant something bad was going to happen. Just being in the mere presence of Larry and Bonnie Ulrey, let alone living within their family, was an honor.

I knew this the moment I walked into their home for the first time and sat at their dinner table.

Bonnie and Larry gave me a real, true feeling of love and acceptance. At this point, the words *Mom* and *Dad* gave me a very high level of anxiety and an uncertain black feeling, never peace. I cannot describe the mixed-up pain I feel when I say that, knowing what that represents with my own mother.

I had been babysitting quite regularly for some time now (and was considered everyone's favorite in my area, because I always cleaned the house and washed dishes before the parents came home) and I had saved up three hundred dollars. Larry noticed my hard work, and one day he announced that if I really wanted a horse, he would pay half.

He took me to the farm one weekend where we had our choice of about twenty horses. I was immediately drawn to a beautiful white one. When I pointed him out, Larry decided it was a good choice, and Rose Bud became my new best friend. I called him Buddy. As soon as we got him home, I happily grabbed my savings and ran to Larry, offering to cover my end of the deal. He promptly held up his hand in a stop-right-there motion and told me to keep my money in my savings account. My horse was a gift from him. I was so excited!

Paula taking Clara for a ride on Buddy

Paula taking Brian for a ride on Buddy

This was shortly after my abortion and Larry's gesture could not have come at a better time. I never rode Buddy with a saddle, preferring to ride bareback. He liked to run like the wind, and I loved to let him go as fast as he could. I know Larry worried when we flew by, but I got such a feeling of freedom with this magnificent and powerful creature under me. Many times I dropped the reins and held my hands high in the air as we ran through the fields. Buddy was very loyal to me and never let me fall.

When I turned sixteen, Bonnie and Larry left the Methodist church they had attended and began attending the Pentecostal Mount Vernon Bible College Chapel. A friend of Bonnie's had told her that there was this terrific youth group there and that she should check it out for me. The Bible College had the best youth group in the area. I became heavily involved in the organization, and I really looked forward to attending each meeting. Some healing even started to take place as I connected my mind, body, and soul together during the praise and worship singing. Although I did become a born-again Christian, I was far from considering myself completely healed. What lurked in my past was not pretty, but finally I felt as though what I was experiencing was more typical of a normal life. I had my new companion, Buddy, and my relationship with my new parents was going well. I had now been in my new home for a of couple years, my sister Sharon lived with me again, and life was good.

Another part of my healing process came from attending the group sessions that Judith Goodhand, director of Knox County Children's Services, led at the Children's Services Center. We were a group of troubled young women from abused and neglected families, and some were rape victims. Judith expected each of us to answer for our own lives and determine how we would handle each problem. She had a great way of gently guiding us to our own conclusions and letting us figure out how to handle our lives. She always assured us that we could call her any time, even at home, if any of us had a crisis. She gave her whole heart to each child. I remember times she would see me coming down the hall and leave a meeting to come see if I was okay or if I needed something. She was truly in her work for the kids.

I remember one crisis in particular, which took place after I had a huge fight with my boyfriend. It started up all kinds of battles in my mind, and I took off across a field at full throttle. My dad, Larry, came running right after me for quite a distance. Then, all of a sudden, he went in the other direction as if he did not even care I was running away. I kept going; I could not keep my mind from replaying the fight with my boyfriend over and over in my head. I was coming up to the next hill and getting out of breath. My legs ached as I pushed myself, and I could barely make out what was ahead of me from the tears in my eyes. Suddenly, I felt someone grab me! It was Larry. He had actually gotten in his car and had driven up the hill to the next road, knowing I was going to end up there. I started screaming and went a bit crazy, but Larry managed to get me home, where I called Judith. I ended up going to her house that night to cool down. Her whole family had the same we-will-fight-for-you attitude as she did. I stayed there until I calmed down. She did not treat me as if I were imposing at all. She was just there for me.

Chapter 8
Meeting Bob

One evening I came home from youth group and there was a note on the table saying, "Do not go anywhere; we have a meeting with Judith at seven." Cold chills ran up my spine. It could mean anything, and with the way the state was changing their rules, it could not be good news. When Bonnie came inside the house, I knew from her expression that something was terribly wrong, but she was not permitted to disclose what the meeting was about.

Bonnie usually was adorned in a nice dress and wore heels when she was out in public, but this time she had just returned in her walking pants, which were full of holes. I knew when I saw her swollen eyes and the way she was dressed that it was not good. Then, when Larry came home, there was no hiding the fact that he was upset. He also had a look and expression as if he had not slept in days.

When we arrived at Judith's office, the people present were Larry and Bonnie, Sharon, Terry, and me, along with my Uncle Larry and Aunt Linda who, as a kinship home, had taken Terry in. Judith began the discussion with a lot of small talk that did not make much sense. She seemed awfully unnerved, which was out of character for her and made me very uneasy.

Forty-five minutes later, we still did not know why we were there. I asked Judith what was going on, and she excused the other four adults in the room and proceeded to tell Sharon, Terry, and me what was happening. Looking into each of our eyes as she spoke, she said, "In fifteen minutes, your birth father, Bob Krohmer, will walk into this room.

"As we speak, he is sitting on the other side of this wall. He's come to Mount Vernon from Atlanta to meet you. We did not want it to happen like this, but there is nothing we can do about it. I have no choice but to introduce you to him and leave you alone for a while." We were so caught off-guard that we were all totally speechless. My thoughts flashed back to a conversation I had had with Judith when I was fourteen, when she had asked me if I ever wanted to meet my biological father. I had told her I would like to meet him some day. Now, in fifteen minutes, he was going to walk through the door. None of us spoke—we just watched the door, in shock that this reunion was actually about to happen with only fifteen minutes' warning.

What would happen when we met this Robert Krohmer? In my birth mother's infinite wisdom, she had called the state for new birth certificates, telling them that she had lost our originals, and had named Dave as our father, to keep us from ever knowing that Robert Krohmer was our birth father. I knew that Uncle Larry and Aunt Linda were very upset with me for even thinking about finding my biological father. All of this was such a disruption for all of our parents as well as for us.

When the door finally opened, it felt as if time were moving in slow motion. I felt my knees shaking and my heart racing, and I tried to control it but could not. All the questions started to take over inside my head, and that roller coaster that I had neatly tucked away reappeared. Our lives had just begun to settle down and now this!

When the man came into the room, he did not open his arms to us. Instead, he seemed ready for a confrontation. I could look at him but not speak. The first thing I looked for was what I remembered as a very small girl, the curly blond hair on his arms. He had the same blond hair on his arms as our other dad, Dave. He was the same height, had the same color hair, eyes, and build—and even his voice sounded the same. My mother's second husband, Dave, looked as if he could be our real father's brother! It was really very strange.

The first thing out of his mouth was that he was currently married to a lady named Diane, and they were very devout Jehovah's Witnesses, down in Atlanta, Georgia. His next sentence stunned all three of us. He said, "I came to Mount Vernon to take you home with me, so you can become members of the congregation." He paused for a moment, and since we were all still silent, he found it a good time to let us know exactly what had happened between him and our mother so many years ago.

He started by saying that when he was transferred to West Germany, he had had to leave my mother, and us, behind. He journeyed home once to visit, but she met him at the door and told him not to come in and "Oh, by the way, I want a divorce." He said he had found his personal belongings in the front yard. He had forced himself into the house and found Dave's things already moved in. It had all seemed like a bad movie.

The next event took me by surprise. When he realized he had been replaced by Dave, they had gotten into a huge fight and a knife was thrown that he was sure went inches past my head. He admitted that he had thrown the knife at my mother out of anger for being replaced. I do not recall this episode. I had been only three years old. Just as he was explaining all of this, Judith came in and told us we had to move our meeting to another location, because the center was closing down for the night. Uncle Larry and Aunt Linda agreed we could meet at their house.

The Ulreys insisted they would drive Sharon and me, while Uncle Larry and Aunt Linda drove Terry. However, Bob Krohmer had other ideas; he wanted us to ride with him. Neither set of parents would allow that, so right away this meeting was off to a catastrophic start. Of course, nobody involved was happy with me for even suggesting that we try to find him in the first place. I was sixteen the night all of this unfolded, and I had been fourteen when I told Judith that I would someday like to meet the guy that called himself my dad.

The reason he was notified was that it was the state's job to locate any and all blood relatives who survived kids that were wards of the State of Ohio. By the look in their eyes, I could tell that everyone involved thought I was a big troublemaker. Before we had even stepped away from the cars in the driveway, there was another loud confrontation between Larry Ulrey and Bob Krohmer. This time, Larry Ulrey was telling Bob he would never let him take his daughters away.

While all of this was going on, we three girls did not know what to do. We had no idea what would happen next; it was truly awful, and moreover, it was very untimely in our lives. As I stood in our uncle's front yard watching this, Linda, Terry's foster mom, started yelling at me, saying, "If your mother knew you caused this, Paula, she would roll over in her grave!" How could I have known two years ago that making the comment about meeting my real father would cause so much chaos! Needless to say, I felt about an inch high.

When we returned home about eleven that night, I walked up the steps to the house. Larry was so quiet, and I knew he was upset about the whole thing. Bonnie was devastated. I had never seen her so upset. I can remember watching her walking slowly up the stairs. Her expression was unexplainable and more troubled than I even knew Bonnie could be. When I went to the doorway of the living room, she was already in her chair with her eyes closed, clutching her Bible. I stood at the entrance to the living room. Part of me wanted to run to her, but I just fell apart. My knees felt like soft noodles as I walked toward her.

I could not have run if I'd wanted to. It only took one glance to know where I needed to be. As scared as I was, I walked over and sat on the heat register and began sobbing. This was my thinking place, and it was five feet across from Bonnie's chair. It was also the warmest place in the house. I was cold in body and soul at this moment. Bonnie put her Bible down, stood up, took a few steps across the floor, and fell to her knees in front of me, embracing me. We cried together for what seemed like an eternity, with her only words being, "It will be okay, Paula."

There were so many unanswered questions, and both Bonnie and I knew that neither of us had the answers. We just rocked back and forth in an embrace. Sharon never came into the room. She headed up the stairs and went to bed without even saying goodnight. She was not a communicator. She always has been, and still is, one to keep most of her thoughts to herself.

For the next two days, members of the Ulrey family came by to visit, and they would gently say, "You do not have to go to Atlanta. You can stay here with us." For the first time since Dave had told us our mother was dead, I felt that I knew where home really was!

It seemed like decades had passed for me between the ages of eleven and sixteen. In the end, all three of us stayed right where we were. We had no intention of leaving the loving families we were now part of.

We contemplated getting to know this man as a friend, not as a father, because we realized we had the very best dads already. Judith Goodhand had somehow arranged for each of us to make our own decision whether to remain in our current homes or to join Bob Krohmer in Atlanta. We did not know at the time how, or if, she would be able to pull this off. None of us wanted to pull up our roots and join this man who claimed to be our father. We held our breaths until we were told we would be allowed to remain where we were; after all, we had finally put down roots for the first time in over four years.

Bob Krohmer turned out to be reasonable, and we agreed to write to each other. We each wrote to him at different times, and he wrote to us. He brought his new family—three children, and his wife, Diane—to Mount Vernon to meet and get to know us. We visited him twice within the next two years in Atlanta. The friendship that developed between the Krohmer family and us was very different.

Bob loved his cigarettes, women, gambling, and alcohol. He was also a man who loved to show off his possessions, such as his big diamonds and Cadillacs. There were things he would ask me to do for him when he came to visit that were just not appropriate, such as line up a girl for him when I picked him up from the airport. I always pretended not to hear him say such things. For goodness' sake, he was married at the time! He liked to talk about intimate things no father should tell his daughter, such as details of his sexual relationship with my mother and their favorite places to make love. He told me my mother was the most passionate lover he had ever known and that there would never be anyone like her.

I believe Bob never stopped loving my mother. Somehow, he had managed to keep a collection of photographs hidden from Diane all those years, and I was so happy when he gave me this cherished stash. Some of the pictures were of me as a tiny baby. Whenever he was in town, he would arrange for me to meet yet another one of his brothers or sisters who still lived in the Cleveland area of Ohio. At the age of thirty-four, I met his mother—or my grandmother, Pauline—for whom I was named. When he talked about Mama, it was if she were still alive and in his arms. Sometimes it raised the hair on the back of my neck to hear him speak of her. I believe when Dave stepped into their marriage and forced him to sign us over to him, a big part of Bob died. It did not matter what happened, though; whenever I saw him, he hugged me as if I had never left.

He talked about how all of that broke his heart and spirit and how he was never the same man afterward. Even with this bizarre relationship we had, when he left from a visit, I always cried. Later in life, when I met his siblings, they would fill me in on some of his childhood turmoil, which might explain the horrible way he treated his body. His drinking and smoking had aged him beyond his years. In July 2001 he needed surgery to repair aortic aneurysms brought on by the smoking. The day before his surgery, his friend took him to the casino to enjoy his favorite pastime of gambling.

That night, he called me to say his good-byes, because the doctors had told him it was unlikely he would survive the surgery. I remember sitting on my couch telling myself that this call was not happening. When I hung up, I dismissed the call, thinking he was most likely out drinking and was just depressed. I was not able to grab the concept that my birth father had just called me and said he would be dying the next day, which is exactly what he did. As the doctors tried to wake him after ten hours of surgery to replace his artery a blood clot went to his brain and he died.

The next evening, at about six o'clock, I received a call from my sister, Terry, who was crying hysterically that "Dad" had died right after coming out of a ten-hour surgery. Up till that moment, I had never heard Terry utter the word "Dad" to refer to Bob Krohmer. He died at the age of sixty. His three daughters attended his funeral in Atlanta, Georgia. The service was as strange as the relationship had been. His most recent wife, Patricia, buried him in her family's private cemetery in the mountains of Georgia. He was buried in his favorite old T-shirt and bathrobe. It was so strange from beginning to end. Only one of his remaining four siblings attended the funeral, and of his six children, five of us were there. My sister Sharon sang the song, "In the Arms of an Angel." At the age of forty one I could not cry. I could not believe how very dysfunctional this burial was. I just felt numb. I sat and remembered the times he had come to Mount Vernon to celebrate the births of his two grandchildren Christina and Adam and just stayed thankful for that. I said my prayer of peace for him, and we all went home in astonishment.

Bob Krohmer with his best friend King, as a 16 year old, and holding Paula as a new baby

Bob bringing new sibs to meet up,
and last visit with him before he passed

Chapter 9
Independence

My grandma, Dave's mother, used to check in with me from time to time after we were placed into foster care, keeping me updated with my former family. I never knew whose side she was really on; sometimes it seemed like ours, but mostly I felt she kept in contact just so she could be Lynn's informant on our whereabouts. I believe Lynn really feared us once we were in the foster care system and given up for unwanted.

During one of Grandma's calls, I inquired about my mother's remains. She told me Dave had had Mama's urn buried at Mound View Cemetery, in Mount Vernon. After that, I would frequently cut school and walk to the cemetery a mile away, stealing a daffodil along the way. The first time I went, I stopped at the cemetery office, where the worker gave me a row number at the back of the cemetery, all the way up an enormous hill, quite far from the office. I wasn't able to find her plot there, so I went back to the office and she sent me in another direction. When I could not find it a second time, I went back to the office again, sick to my stomach and sobbing, but she sent me away to look in yet another area.

I kept going back to the cemetery; each time I was sure I would soon stumble upon her name on a marker. I would just walk and cry. It was the only time I truly allowed myself to feel the anger that I still carried about the lack of control around my mother's death. Sometimes I got tired and sat to rest beside one of the tall tombstones. Occasionally I would fall asleep and wake up still holding the flower I had brought. I would usually just place it on a nearby grave and leave. I did this for the first year during the turmoil of all the changing foster homes. This was not something ordinary that you would tell the average person about. So I kept this to myself and never told anyone. To tell would mean I would have to talk about my confusion and pain.

I still have commonly recurring memories of all the horrible things Dave said to us girls about killing our mother. It left me confused and always wondering if we really had. I walked around feeling guilty and wondering how, or if, we really had somehow killed her. It was a daunting feeling to carry around during those very impressionable years. When you are told something over and over as a young child, it becomes a part of your truth. I am not sure if your inner child really ever sorts it out. At the age of fifty, I still drift back to those thoughts.

A year after I moved in with the Ulrey family, Judith Goodhand asked Terry, Sharon, and me if we wanted to return home to live with Dave. We all asked the same question at the same time: "Is Lynn still there?" When the answer was yes, we all refused to ever go back. Our wishes were granted, because Judith arranged it so we would never have to return to the house we all knew as "hell."

Soon after Dave's surrender and abandonment was made permanent, Larry Ulrey posed his desire to adopt Sharon and me. He already frequently called me "daughter number two" and Sharon was "daughter number three." By this time, however, I had already been adopted once by Dave and had been through seven foster homes, so the last thing I wanted was to be adopted again. In my mind, being adopted still did not mean security, and there was always a chance that I could be given away again. I refused his proposal, and Sharon followed suit. We did not know at the time how painful it was for Larry and Bonnie to be turned down—but they were unaware just how deep our pain, anger, and insecurities ran.

My sister Terry was able to escape her pain by reading novels. She could read a book in a day to escape the reality that she was alone without Sharon and me. She told me she frequently would get into trouble for reading too much. She would take a flashlight to bed and read under the covers. Even though Terry lived with Dave's brother, our "uncle," I think she still never felt as loved or as wanted in her foster home as Sharon and I did. When she shared some of the secrets about her life, Sharon and I would get so angry and cry out for someone to bring her home with us to the Ulreys.

It never happened. At sixteen, I realized I was going to have to make some pretty substantial decisions. I was becoming independent and making choices that would affect the rest of my life. The Ulreys and Judith were supporting me through all of them, and they were always a source of comfort. Judith started involving me and encouraged me to become active in the administrative side of foster care. I became involved in making videos, in an effort to help change the laws for the betterment of foster kids and to aid in the training of new foster parents. I participated in panel discussions that allowed new foster-parent trainees to ask me questions. Sometimes these questions were personal and intimate, but I tried to answer honestly so it would help them better understand their prospective foster kids.

It was an honor to explain how it feels to walk into a home you have never been to before and suddenly be asked to blend in with this new family, where there are brothers, sisters, parents, and pets. I also explained about feeling inadequate about knowing the "rules" of the family. At Larry and Bonnie's house, talking on the phone was a big deal; other places it wasn't. (I would have talked for hours if they had let me). When I disobeyed Larry, he would just point to the rules and then praise one of my best qualities. I like his old-school attitude: if you cannot say anything nice, do not say anything at all.

I also talked to the prospective foster parents about how hard it is for a foster kid to talk with their new foster parents about sensitive issues. One of my biggest topics was to the new parents: I tried my hardest to make sure they knew how important it was to always be the one to orient the new kids and not to let the other kids in the home do the orienting. I stood my ground on that and many other notes when it came to helping the new parents get ready to receive their first foster children. I mentioned issues like my chronic "female problems" being severe at times; that was a subject that many girls had a hard time sharing with new family members. Many times, these panel discussions brought tears as well as a few laughs. The caseworkers seemed to be as caught off-guard as were the potential foster parents. Even though it was sometimes quite painful for me to speak openly about my experiences, I healed from it. It was always calming to me to know that ultimately it would make the lives of the kids entering the foster-care system easier—as well as the lives of the parents.

When the center's first new girl's group home opened, Judith invited me to sit in the group-therapy sessions once a week to act as the "ex-foster girl." At first the girls did not accept me, but after I had shared some of what I had survived, they soon came to accept and trust me. Many of the girls would tell me that they would rather go through their experiences over again than have to experience mine! They were in a group-home environment because of delinquency issues, something I did not really have in common with them. It did not matter; after each session with these girls, I felt very protected and safe. It eventually started to seem as if God were smiling down on me. He was giving me the very kind support of the child-care system and, of course, Judith herself. She kept me under her wing and shared with me a wealth of knowledge that would eventually bring me to this position where I could help guide not only the future foster parents and youth but the case managers that struggled with their own issues.

One of the hardest things in school had been the label of "foster child." I struggled, as did other foster children and children of adversity, with bullying to the nth degree. When the first word got out in the junior high school that I was a foster child, my peers automatically assumed that I was there because I was a troubled delinquent. Their stalking and name-calling sometimes became so overwhelming that school became a dreaded place—but I was still hoping that I would run into one of my siblings in the halls, so I just tolerated it.

The girls were so cruel, they would come at me by groups of ten to twenty, sometimes taunting me and calling me a variety of names. I had become so good at staying at a distance from all of my peers to avoid this bullying that I appeared to be a loner or unsociable. All of my time at junior high and into early high school I was simply petrified. I was pushed, spit on, and had food and paint from the art room thrown at me; I was jabbed with pencils, accused of unthinkable things, cornered in the girls' locker room, and pushed into lockers. While I was in the showers after gym, the girls would take my clothes, leaving me in the shower with a mere towel—and sometimes I was lucky to get that. I learned quickly to take my clothes into the shower. I was given the nickname of "Miss America," and no matter where I went within the school, I was mocked with this label. The teachers never knew the deep fear I felt when they forced us out onto the school grounds for gym or lunch.

My life seemed like a revolving door during the times with various new families and foster homes. It was so hard for me to talk to these new parents about what was happening to me each day at school. I so feared going into the restroom during the changing of classes or during gym time that many days I would go the entire school day without using the restroom. It was daunting waiting that long during my days of the month—which I did not know how to even talk about to a teacher or parent. If I used the restroom at school, I would have to make a spectacle of myself and ask to be excused right in the middle of the class, hoping and praying there would be no other girls in the restroom. There were days I barely made it home without urinating in my pants.

I tolerated this without discussing it with a new parent until about my junior year. This girl named Becky had been telling the whole lunch room and gym class that I was calling her home every night and asking for her dead brother. One day I ran out of the cafeteria to stand outside; the anger from her taunting me with this morbid lie was upsetting me so much that my stomach was upset. I didn't think I would make it outside without throwing up. I knew I could not go to the restroom and take the chance that she and all of her "friends" might follow me.

I had reached the fresh air outside and barely got myself together, when she jumped into my face and shouted out in front of all the other kids outside, "I should take those glasses off your face and shove them down your throat!" It was then that something snapped in me, and I whipped them off my face and shoved them into hers, telling her to go ahead and do it! I was so shocked and disgraced by her lies that I could no longer hold the anger back. I had taken enough from my heartless school peers. It got heated, and I would not back down from her. My adrenalin was so far out of control, and I had taken so much for such a long time, that I could not hold back from wanting to make her eat my glasses. The next thing I knew, the school cop, Wendall, grabbed my arm and pulled me to the principal's office.

It took this explosion to force me to talk to Larry about what this girl and so many others had been doing to me for so long. The next day, he took me to school and straight into the principal's office to get the matter straightened out. I thought that I would be the one reprimanded, and not Becky. By the time Larry Ulrey left the office that morning, the tide had turned, and Becky was the one to get reprimanded. This lesson taught me that, no matter what had happened, communicating this bullying with my new dad did pay off! The offenses I had suffered for years had gone too far and jeopardized so much for me. They affected not only my grades but also my dignity within the school community. To this day, it is sometimes hard for me to even say "High School Reunion," let alone go to one! What officials do not seem to understand is that there is an unwritten rule: "Don't tell your parents or anyone" when these offenses are going on. It was hard for me to talk about it, but when I was dragged to the principal's office and had to make it right with my parents, it forced me to talk. For me, my dad was my hero.

My hope in sharing this rather difficult time of my life is that any parent reading this will understand the importance when a typically quiet child, who never gets into trouble, one day, out of the blue, ends up in the principal's office. This is a huge red flag. I would have died before getting into trouble and ending up there. For me, it worked out; for some, it makes it much worse. It could have ended much worse, because by the time this nightmare exploded, if there had not been a school cop on the grounds, I believe I would have made this girl eat those glasses—as she had taunted she was going to do to me. I probably would have hurt her and been in more trouble than I could have dealt with, on top of the other adversities I was already navigating.

www.k12.com

www.talk-helps.com

www.mcgruff.org

www.bullybusters.org

www.jodeeblanco.com
www.haltabuse.org
www.mysafesurf.org

During the blizzard of 1978, I was a junior in high school, and I found out I was pregnant again—this time by the young man I had been dating for over a year. When I dropped this bomb on Bonnie and Larry, they were understandably shocked, and we all said things we shouldn't have. Immediately, though, one thing was established. This man would marry me and make it right. Larry would see to it that he honored me and yet another baby would not be aborted.

We also agreed that, no matter what, I would graduate from high school. Even though we were so young to be starting a family, Jay and I were not unhappy about having this child. We were actually very excited about it. I was very in love with Jay, or as in love as a wounded teenager could be. While I was carrying his baby, it was one of the happiest times of my life, certainly up until then. We married on March 4, 1978, and I was officially emancipated from the foster-care system. I was now my own legal guardian! But I had no idea what was ahead of me and what was still lurking from my past. I still had too many raw emotions for me to be bringing a child into the world. I was still a child myself. I was the last person that needed to be married; I needed to first resolve some issues from my past.

Unfortunately, no one could tell me that—and if they had, it wouldn't have mattered, because I was focused on a new life that no one could take away. My pregnancy was perfect. Together, Jay and I managed to start a home in a little tiny apartment in Mount Vernon. The apartment was painted with those '70s bright-colored flowers on the kitchen cabinets. I still smile when I remember the brilliant aqua-blue background behind the wildly colorful flowers. We both loved this tiny little one-bedroom apartment, and best of all, I was only about four miles from Larry and Bonnie.

Bonnie stayed very involved with me throughout my pregnancy, making sure I had everything a new mother needed—plus! She helped my transition into motherhood be more magical by preparing me and making sure that I had everything a baby needed. I knew she was worried when she talked with me. It had been many years since she had experienced what I was going through. Bonnie created a 101 crash course to prepare me for young motherhood over a six-month period. There was not a day of my pregnancy that she was not there schooling me on what I would require to be a new mother.

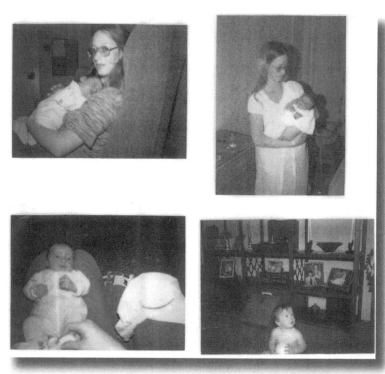

Paula at 17, new mom of Christina Ann 9/1978

My daughter, Christina Ann, was born on September 21, 1978. The labor was only five hours long. She almost arrived before the doctor did. She was a bouncing eight pounds and seven ounces and was twenty-one inches long. She had the loudest cry in the nursery, which would be remembered for a long time. I wanted to give my new daughter the best start in life, so I alerted the hospital staff that I would be breastfeeding. The nurses tried to talk me out of it because of my age and because I was still in school. Again, I felt as if nobody thought I was capable of doing anything right.

This made me even more determined that I could, and would, do the right thing with my new baby. The nurse, who tried endlessly to talk me out of breastfeeding, brought my little girl to me for the first time and said she was hungry; then she left without giving me any instructions on how to nurse a baby. Alone in the room, I held her close, as I had seen in the pictures, and it became one of the most natural and easiest things I have experienced. I never had a problem with nurturing that new little life. I enjoyed every sense of being a mom, from nursing, to washing cloth diapers, to making my own baby food. Being a mom came very easily for me. I was the healthiest and happiest I could ever remember being in my whole life.

I was convinced that Christina would never know the abuse and neglect that I knew growing up. Bonnie was there for many years to come, to help me and to also nurture Christina as a grandmother would do. Her dad was a good person. He somehow always managed to pay the bills and put food on the table, but we eventually realized we were both just too young to be married, and we were both still tending the wounds from our pasts. We honored our agreement of never hurting our child—as our parents had with us. When Christina was two and a half years old, we divorced, but we continued to treat each other with respect, and we still remain friends.

One summer day, out of the blue, my grandma (Dave's mother) called to say that Dave was bringing the twins into town for a visit. She invited the three of us to come see them. My heart leapt with joy! They were nine years old now. The last time I had seen them they had been only six and standing in the driveway as we were being taken away by the caseworkers. Larry let Sharon and me borrow his Ford LTD for the reunion. We drove about twenty miles; we were so anxious that it seemed like one hundred!

When I got to Grandma's mobile home in the little town of Homer, the twins ran out and jumped into the car. They were not about to let us get out and come in the house, nor would we have wanted to. Debbie looked up into my eyes with a pain I recognized. She had the saddest expression on her face. She did not want to say anything, but I could tell she was scared and upset by what was going on in her household. Deon would not even look up; she just kept staring at the floor. She would not talk at all throughout our whole visit. I could see tears rolling down her face, but no matter how much I tried to get her to talk, she just had a blank look on her face, showing no expression. This reminded me of my mother!

I was frightened, and the anxiety welled up in me to the point that I wanted to run into the trailer and just choke my stepmother, whom I could see was peeking at us through the blinds. I knew the twins were scared of what lay ahead after this visit. Debbie asked me if we still knew the ladies that had come for us years ago. I asked her what she meant, and she said it was bad at home with Lynn, and she wanted those ladies to come and take her and Deon too.

The girls were looking out of the car, watching Grandma's windows to see if Lynn was looking. While sitting in Larry's Ford LTD in Grandma's driveway, both twins continued to become more uneasy and upset. Debbie said Lynn was taking pills and not acting right. She was scared to go back into the mobile home. I asked what she meant, and she started sobbing and pleaded for me to call those ladies before it was too late. She said Lynn was hitting both of them all the time, and they might not last much longer. As soon as I returned home that evening, I called Judith Goodhand. I told her of Debbie's plea for help.

Judith advised me of how to make an anonymous referral to Children's Services, and she sternly reminded me that I was never to admit to anyone that I had made the referral. She assured me it would remain confidential, and I would be protected.

About two weeks later, Grandma called again, asking me to stay by the phone because Dave was going to call me soon. She said he was upset and wanted to talk to me about something important. I panicked and called Judith. I told her I was not sure, but I suspected he was calling about the referral. Judith agreed, and told me not to answer the phone until she got there. I was not surprised to find that, in the middle of the work week, past eight-thirty in the evening, Judith would be there, once again, to help me through this latest catastrophe. At this time in my life I was eighteen, and my baby was about three months old, but Judith was still there for me.

She arrived as the phone was ringing and went into my bedroom to get on the extension as I answered in the kitchen. For the first time, she was hearing the voice of the true monster I had always described to her. My body was breaking out in hives from head to toe, and tears began pouring down my face when I heard his voice.

Dave started out by asking me who had turned him in for child abuse of the twins. I looked up to see Judith motioning for me not to admit anything. Through the open door she could see the look on my face as the conversation got worse. It felt so safe knowing she was there to protect me. Her presence, however, did not make the pain inside my heart any less at hearing his voice after all this time. He told me anything the twins said about Lynn was lies, and he told me that I was only telling people this because I was still mad about being put into a foster home.

He began accusing me and my sisters of killing our mother (again, after all these years), and he even blamed us for her shock-therapy treatment the last time she had been hospitalized. He kept asking me if I had turned him in, but I denied it each time. He said if I did not tell him who had turned him in he would come to Mount Vernon and kick my ass all over town until I did.

At that point, Judith interrupted the conversation, saying into the phone, "Dave, did I just hear you threaten your daughter with physical abuse?" Then she walked into the kitchen, took the phone out of my hand, and hung it up. I was five foot seven inches to her petite five foot two, but I knew she meant business when she said, "Don't pick up that phone!" She walked back into my bedroom, leaving me in the kitchen, and shut the door. As I held my daughter, through the door I heard Judith speaking very calmly, almost in a monotone. Not once did she raise her voice.

Depending on who you speak with, Judith is a caring, compassionate advocate for "her" foster kids—or she is a strong-willed, fierce adversary who can intimidate just by walking into a room. Coming out of the bedroom, she said, "You do not ever have to worry about that man again as long as you live. I will take care of him." Then she hugged me, reassured me I had done the right thing, and walked out my door. It felt as though she had scooped up all the fear I'd ever felt and taken it with her. She had made me feel she had the monster by the tail. Later, through obtaining copies of the court records, I found out she really had taken care of it. It was not long before I held court papers that showed one count of neglect for each one of us girls.

Chapter 10
Twice Bitten

I met a man named Patrick. We were introduced at his brother Chris's twenty-first birthday party. Chris's wife, Althea, had invited me to tag along after work one night. Althea and I both worked at a little fast-food chain. Patrick was twenty-seven years old and I was twenty. He had never been married; he ran the family dairy farm. We found ourselves walking away from the party while everyone else was getting drunk. We sat on his brother's porch and talked most of the night. We talked about his family, the animals on the farm, and how his entire family worked together to make the farm successful. I was impressed and interested to know that the family was so close.

He captured my attention, and we began to date soon after that party. This went on for a year, and we did everything together, from work to play. He gave me the opportunity to enjoy being on the farm. I soon had a great desire to roll up my sleeves and get dirty and smelly; I was happy to work beside him from dawn till dusk. At first, I just loved the whole farm family life. Through it, I came to realize that I was a real country girl! Although many would call it work, I felt that working with the animals was like playing. It was a wondrous journey for me to see all of the animals and the births of the new babies on the farm. My daughter, Christina, was about two years old by now, and she found it all as heavenly as I did. She loved the kitties, puppies, and new baby calves on the farm.

Christina and the Farm

It was a delight to watch her amazement at all the wonders on the farm. She would entertain herself for hours at a time, quietly enjoying Mother Nature. She loved Patrick and he loved her. Watching him teach her was precious. One of my first memories— one I will never forget—was watching her playing on the front porch of the farmhouse with a new litter of six-week-old kittens. She was drawn to a little white kitten in the litter and would never put it down. She would walk around the farm with it tucked under her arm. You would have thought it was a stuffed animal, but it flopped around as she moved, never fighting her to let it down. I could not help but smile while she kept the patient little kitten in her possession all day long.

One day I looked out the door to make sure she was still on the porch and safe, when I noticed something about the kitten that did not look normal. It was no longer flopping with her movements. As I approached the door, she was moving around ordering the other kittens to get into their box. I very quietly asked her to let me hold the white kitten, and when she handed it to me, there was no floppiness left in the kitten. It was so sad that it brought tears to my eyes. She must have carried that dead kitten for hours. Puzzled, I glanced down, looking for the other kittens. The remaining four kittens were in their cardboard box. I noticed that the heavy, dirt-filled, wooden flower box had been knocked over. I asked her how the box had fallen, and she just shrugged her shoulders and returned my question with "Can I have my kitten back?" I saw that the kitten's body had been smashed, apparently under the flower box. This was her first lesson of "kitty heaven." It was a very sad lesson, and with her highly unusual photographic memory, we did not stop talking about that kitten for the next year. She had a million questions and would wake me many times at night, crying and asking me where her kitten was.

Another animal story that sticks in my mind took place one day when we were driving down one of the brick roads in Mount Vernon. This was during the time that kids did not have to be in a car seat. I never owned a car seat. Christina was standing in the front seat beside me, just gabbing on at a hundred miles a minute, when a squirrel ran under the car, and we heard a *thump, thump.* She instantly turned her body around to face the road behind us, screaming, "Mommy, stop, stop! You hit a squirrel, and it is dancing in the street!" Her panicked little screaming voice was out of control. I assured her that it would stop dancing and asked her to turn around to make sure no other squirrels would run out in front of the car. She bought it, and to my surprise, it worked. From that day forward, she watched carefully, so that I did not hit another squirrel.

That same day we were on our way back to the farm and were passing an Amish farm. One of their roosters ran out in front of us. I was driving a Volkswagen Rabbit, and of course, just as she had finally settled down from the squirrel, I hit the rooster. While I listened to her shrieking, feathers were flying everywhere, just like a fresh snow! While I was still in amazement that I could hit two animals in the same day, the daughter of the family that owned the rooster came out to see what had happened. I had stopped the car and was watching her walking down the hill. When she realized what all the excitement and screeching of tires was about, she simply picked up the dead rooster and proceeded to chop off its head!

Poor Christina was hysterical by now. She just did not understand any of what she had witnessed that day. On or near the farm, there was always a new experience to be learned, and there was never a dull moment. It got to the point where she watched the men butcher a cow or pig without blinking.

By the end of our first year of dating, Patrick won my heart when he surprised me with an orphaned six-week-old kitten. The new kitten was the same color and had unusual long hair just like the stuffed animal I had called "Puff" while still living under Dave's roof. I was not aware of how attached to the stuffed animal I had been before Dave sent us away. This was one of the first triggers from my past that brought up deep hidden feelings that I was not aware still existed.

Looking back, I see this was leftover *post traumatic childhood stress* from years gone by. Up until the first moment when he brought the kitten in, I had completely blocked that stuffed animal out of my mind and heart. None of the other kittens or cats on the farm had had this effect on me. When I look back at the moment he handed the small fluffy kitten to me, I recall getting teary eyed as I remembered the little friend I had left behind.

Who really knows why; maybe it was just to survive from one minute to the next through the sudden trauma of being jerked from the world I knew into a new world of mass confusion and futile tears. I had blocked that kitten from my mind until this new kitten was placed into my hand. Instantly, with the touch of the fur of my new kitten, I remembered cuddling my stuffed animal every night after horrific things had happened to me. The kitten had allowed me to relax my tightly squinted closed eyes and get a couple hours of sleep. I remember realizing that my eyes could relax and just praying that *she* would not enter my room and work me over.

Christina and Puff

It was like flipping very fast through many pages of a masterfully written horror flick. Patrick thought I was crying because I was happy, but in my mind I was having flashbacks of this forgotten stuffed animal. I realized that I had been really attached to that little fluffy stuffed animal in the past, and I felt very sad that I had forgotten her. I named the new kitten Puff, just as I had named my stuffed animal. By then it had been eight years since I had been within the reach of my dad, Dave, and awful stepmother, Lynn.

What a revelation that moment was. The kitten was soft and gentle, but it brought back memories of the many nights that I had held my stuffed animal and shook after enduring Dave or Lynn's physical or mental abuse. It was then that I realized they had not packed my stuffed animal in the grocery bag they sent me off with.

Suddenly I had a live version of something, and I didn't understand. It wasn't until that glorious magical moment when Patrick handed me my new friend that I had subconsciously realized a missing link. It was as if my mind had allowed me to instantly remember back to that time. It made me realize that the stuffed animal had been one of the only reasons I was able to sleep at all. I had always watched my bedroom door, waiting for a viperous visitor to enter my room and take all of her frustrations out on me. I had developed disturbing sleep problems; to this day I cannot sleep for more than a few hours at a time. At the age of fifty now, I call these memories "leftovers."

I had not thought about those feelings for a very long time. This was the first time I had a flash from the past that shook me up. I could only walk away, shut myself in the bathroom, and cry as I held this little live version of my Puff. It was the first time in a very long time that I had shaken, cried, laughed, and felt sick all at the same time.

I fell in love with Patrick in the instant he put this little kitten in my hands. Somehow, in his own rough country-boy way, he knew I needed that kitten. Christina fell in love with Puff at first sight, and the questions about the white kitten went away. She would say, "Puff is my kitty," and soon we had fourteen cats. We always welcomed more kittens, and we had enough milk from the dairy to keep them happy. What a dream come true! Patrick soon knew that I was not on the farm with him only for a place to live. He had nothing, but yet he had everything. He taught me, as a father would teach his child, about every facet of farm living.

He was very patient when we were in our first year of courting and learning about each other. There were happy feelings, with all the wonders of nature, and there were sad experiences with the animals. When something went wrong, we would lean on each other and be strong for each other. We fell into a world of love. A year or so after meeting Patrick, I was in the hospital recovering from still another surgery related to my female health problems, when my doctor told me that time was running out for me to have more children. If I wanted another baby, I would have to do it soon, because he was running out of ways to repair my reproductive organs. I did not want my little girl to grow up without at least one sibling. Patrick and I decided to get married and start trying for a child right away.

I gave up my little apartment, and together we moved out to the farm. The farm was about twenty miles out of Mount Vernon, in a little town called Amity. I lived on the farm with Patrick, near his brother and parents. There were three houses, all about a mile apart. Our farm was the dairy farm, which brought in more than half of the money the farm generated. His brother lived on the farm that contained the sheep, and his father and mother lived on the farm with the beef herd. It wasn't long before I ceased to be an honored wife and became a farmhand. Patrick warned me against ever trying to get out of the farm chores. I obeyed, partly out of fear and partly because I wanted to be an honored wife again. I assisted in milking the cows twice a day, right up until the night I had my son.

During all of the hours that I worked in the barn helping Patrick, my little Christina sat in the doorway of the milk parlor and watched me work. Sometimes she would go into the other part of the barn where the young calves were and just stand and talk to them, shaking a stick as if she were a schoolteacher instructing them. By now she was three. I worked as hard as Patrick every day. Besides dairy chores, I helped pull bales of hay off the backs of loaded wagons and put the forty-pound hay bales onto elevators. They would go to the loft of the barn to be stored for the winter. Regardless of the weather, I rode standing on the flatbed wagon each evening, while Patrick drove the tractor, throwing bales of hay off the wagon out to the herd of dairy cows.

The herd had outgrown the pastures and needed the extra food each night. As long as I remained a submissive farm hand, the family kept buying more cows to bring in more money. They knew Patrick did not like the milking. Soon after we'd met, the family increased the herd from twenty-eight cows to about sixty-five cows, and there were always about fifteen calves at any given time. The days grew longer and longer with each new addition to the herd. Rain, snow, or sunshine, we were out in the weather earlier each day and later each evening to keep up with all the new additions to the herd. Christina enjoyed it and would often ride on the front of the tractor with Patrick, and she would sit in the milk house on her little green lawn chair, watching us milking the cows. When I look back, I see that she always had a favorite kitten on her lap. In the beginning of Patrick's managing the farm, his mother had struck a deal with him, telling him it was a temporary job. One of his other brothers ran the farm until he became ill and could no longer do the work.

Patrick did not tell me this until after we were married. He was getting angrier about having to be tied to a dairy herd. Dairy farmers can never just pick up and do things for fun. The dairy life makes it critical to stay close to the herd at all times. It seemed that we were always watching out for a cow in trouble during birthing, and it was a must that they be milked twice a day, preferably every twelve hours. There was no such thing as taking a vacation. We never went too far from home. The oldest of the Yoder Amish family next door to the farm became my best friend. She would fill in for me once in a while we had sick or troubled times. Orpha and I became quite close. She was always a "yell" away when I needed her to help fill in. A trip to a fast-food drive-through to get lunch on Sunday became our family outing. We would drive to a department store and sit in the car in the parking lot to eat. This became my weekly date with my husband.

Patrick would never go in and eat anywhere. This lifestyle seemed to make his anger surface, and it continued to grow worse. He was not happy being so tied to the farm. My stupidity—or wanting to please him so much—began one night when I knew Patrick wouldn't be in from the fields until late. Remembering every step from watching him for the last year, I assembled the milking system and had all sixty-five cows milked before he arrived back at our farm to start the evening chores. I had watched everything he did from start to finish for an entire year, in hopes that one day I could do it by myself. I did it all, from assembling the system, milking, and cleaning the system, to taking it apart when I was finished. After I was done with that, I fed the twenty calves with mixed milk and bottles. All the while, I was being assisted by my little helper, with glee on her little face, always ready to hold a bottle for a new baby calf.

When Patrick came home, I could see that he was so tired that he didn't care whether the cows got milked or not. I told him not to worry, because milking was finished, from start to finish. Like a proud peacock, while actually patting myself on the chest, I told him I had done it for him! The look of amazement pleased me. I was so happy that I could be useful to him. Finally, someone needed me! The cows became quieter with me handling them, and the production of milk increased very quickly. The cows did not fear me, but they knew his anger well. He was very quick to take a club, or bar, and clobber one if it even moved the wrong way. The parlor floor would always be wet from their urine while they were being milked, so it was always slippery.

Many times Patrick would chase them around, yelling and swinging some object at them. I would be standing there, scared to death of his anger, trying to get out of their way when they started running toward me. Many times they would slip on the floor and fall onto their backs, with their legs going all directions, and it would kill me inside to see these animals upset. I began to know each one of the cows and their unique personalities. I had watched each of them for a whole year and thought of them as family. There were calm, dependable cows, and there were nasty, kicking cows. I knew when their ears laid back on their necks that *he* was just a few steps away. They would get nervous and start dancing around while locked into their milking places. Patrick got worse and worse as the months went by. I enjoyed what I did in the barn with the animals, especially bottle- or bucket-feeding the baby calves after the other chores were finished. I knew every cow by name, and they came into the milking parlor and usually into the same place each time to be locked in for the milking. This made them safer for anyone milking them. They were large Holsteins, and they felt more protected in their little milking stalls. There were eight places in the parlor. Four cows would be milked at one time and then the milking units would be switched to the other four cows. Often I sang to them (not so prettily, I might add), and the milk output became more than the family had ever seen. They paid me twenty dollars a week to milk the cows, which usually covered the expense of groceries.

We started trying for a child in September, and by February I was pregnant. The family did not have any health insurance for me, so they strongly suggested that we could save money by delivering this child at home. My mother-in-law had the name of a midwife who would consider delivering our baby. It was, of course, hush-hush to have a baby at home, and we were told not to advertise this, since at the time it was not legal to have a baby at home in Ohio. We traveled to a town called Granville to meet Jane (the midwife) when I was about six months pregnant. It was like an interview, to meet and see if this was a good match for her and for us. Patrick and I and Jane agreed that this home birthing was the right thing to do. I asked my good friend, Mary Jo, who had been a dear friend since middle school, if she would assist during the birth. At the time, all I knew was that she knew how to take a blood pressure. Something told me I needed at least that much. She was anxious, and even though she was a little scared, she agreed to do this for me. She stayed on standby until I knew it was time. When Christina heard me have the first real pain, she started crying and asked Patrick if she could go to the other farm with Grandma Pat. She was scared and confused about what was happening, and at the age of four, she made up her mind that she was not going to watch this experience. We did not press the issue, and Patrick's mother came over and picked her up.

She remained with her Grandmother until we called to have her brought back. After twenty-five hours of horrible labor, I knew something was not right and voiced my concern. By then, it was too late to try to get to a hospital. It was a very frigid November night. There was knee-deep snow, and it was too bad to drive in the snowstorm. During the night, Patrick and Mary Jo were falling asleep. I knew my labor was not progressing as Christina's labor had. Jane did not want to be called until I was sure I was in the late stage of labor, so we waited. I remember being so anxious wondering if she would even be able to get there when we finally did call her. She would be driving an hour to get to the farm.

While Patrick and Mary Jo slept, I took a flashlight and walked through the pasture fields, up and down the hills. I only prayed that the walk would help jump-start the labor and make it move a little faster. I was scared out of my mind, but I was determined to make my husband and in-laws happy by having this baby at home. This way there would be no worry about a hospital bill. My labor started at 7:00 p.m. on November tenth, and my son was born at 2:20 p.m. on November twelfth. We did not know the sex of this child until the moment of his birth. I remember Mary Jo screaming about how much hair he had. When he was finally born, I felt relief to know that Patrick now had the son he had always dreamed about.

Right after the baby was born, our real problems began. I started to hemorrhage when the placenta would not deliver. I was bleeding profusely. The only people in the house were my very best friend, Mary Jo; my husband, Patrick; and the midwife, Jane. As I remained on a mattress on the floor, bleeding heavily, they feverishly tried to keep up with the amount of blood escaping my body. They scurried about, screaming and running all over trying to find towels to soak up all the blood. Soon I could no longer hear their screaming words, and a feeling of peace came over me. I recall how silly they looked carrying on, and I was silently laughing at them. I had lost so much blood so fast from the delivery that I could no longer feel anything, smell anything, or hear anything.

Although I was alert enough to know that something was very wrong, I did not feel afraid. I told myself that since God had let me survive everything in my past, surely He would let me live through this. I felt safe, and I kept trying to tell everyone to settle down. I was all right. I prayed, "God, I promised you many years ago, through blood sweat and tears, that if you let me have my own children, I would never let anyone hurt them. If one of us has to go, let it be me." As I watched Jane letting Patrick cut the umbilical cord, she lifted my new baby onto my belly so I could finally meet my beautiful little boy. I was amazed at the head full of black satin hair and how his eyes looked right into mine. His skin was blue from the long, hard labor, but his heartbeat was strong. I put my hand on his back to feel him breathe, and his legs and arms seemed to be moving normally. I grabbed one of his hands and felt his strong grip. His first look into my eyes made them flood with tears.

Feeling his weight and size on my belly, I knew he would be just fine. Although my son was doing well, I was experiencing an extreme loss of blood from hemorrhaging and could feel myself slipping away. I asked them to take him off me because I was having such a hard time breathing. I have fond memories of watching Mary Jo holding him and then Patrick taking him and sitting in the rocking chair, just adoring him.

Meanwhile, Mary Jo did as Jane instructed, but I could see in her expression that I was not the only one worried. Before the delivery, I'd told everyone that, no matter what, I wanted to put the first diaper and outfit on the baby. When Adam was about two hours old, they helped me by holding me upright so that I could dress him. I felt the blood flowing way too fast and realized I really was not fine, but I had a need to make sure both of my children were.

They brought Christina back from her grandma's house, and she sat in her little rocking chair by the mattress on the floor where Adam had been born and held her new little brother. I was relieved as I thought, *At least she has a little brother.* My husband took the baby to the doctor. We had an agreement with our family doctor that he would see the baby as soon as he was born. This would be the well-baby checkup. I remained on the mattress, shaking, trembling, and hemorrhaging for over a week. No doubt I was in shock. Meanwhile, the midwife, Jane, kept shooting 180-proof alcohol down my throat, believing that it would keep me from dying. Her intentions were good, but I'm sure this actually promoted the blood loss.

Christina holding Adam 11/1982 when he was 2 hours old

At the time, I never realized how close to death I really was. No one came to visit for the first week except Bonnie and Aunt Linda. Bonnie was very upset and tried to talk me into going in town with her to the doctor, but I refused. The thought of leaving my new son was horrifying to me, and I already knew that my doctor had rules against me delivering the baby at home. His exact words had been, "Paula you do not have my blessing to try to do something this foolish; you have already had too many surgeries, and you are more than high-risk." I did not tell anyone about this conversation before or after this home birth experience. I know that when Bonnie saw me, the hair that had not already been gray turned gray. She knew more than I was telling her; she knew me like a book. When she came into the house that day, I did not move. I feared that I would disappoint everyone in Patrick's family, but I feared more disappointing Bonnie. I did not tell anyone how bad this situation was. I just focused on getting well quickly, so that I could take care of my new baby and my daughter.

The thought of being whisked off to the hospital was almost morbid to me. I did not want anyone to know that my world had almost come to an end. In my mind I just wanted everything to go back to what I knew as normal. Later, after Patrick had returned from the doctor's office with Adam, he announced that our son had weighed in at eight pounds and seven ounces. Still in shock I asked him, "I lost a lot of blood didn't I?" His reply was that he had seen cows bleed more than I bled.

Patrick and his family never took me to the doctor. Six weeks later I saw my doctor, and he looked over his glasses at me the entire time he was examining me. Dr. Fairchild had doctored me since I was fifteen years old, piecing me back together during many emergency surgeries. If a look could slap me upside my head, his did, that day. He said to me, "Paula, I do not know how you made it through this alive, but you managed—congratulations on your new son." He helped me sit up before he left. I left feeling a sort of chill but happy that all was well.

I soon realized the notion that I had married a gentle man and his close-knit family was a fantasy. Shortly after Adam was born, my new husband began to exhibit deep, hostile feelings. He felt that his parents had trapped him into farming. He had no desire to be a farmer, especially a dairy farmer. He went to bed angry every evening and woke up angry every morning. His father seemed to dictate our whole schedule. His fighting with his parents started to affect our marriage, and things got worse every day. Adam was growing up fast, while times were getting tougher and tougher between his father and me.

Adam was always very active, looking for something to get into. He was a Curious George, and by the time he was three there was not a thing on that farm that he did not have his hand into. He knew where everything was, and he was very good at asking about it even when he knew he was not allowed to get into it. One day I remember taking my eyes off him for one short minute. When I looked back, he was gone! Both his sister and I set out on a hunt-for-Adam crusade. Running as quickly as we could around and into every nook of the farm, we finally found him outside, up on the largest tractor on the farm, saying, "Look, Mommy, I'm driving!" He always wore his little black "hunting hat," as he called it.

Adam and the Farm

Another instance was when he set a wax bear figure on the upstairs kerosene heater. He yelled down the stairs, "Mommy, I think I am in trouble," and right after that he yelled, "Am I going get my butt smacked?" I ran to the foot of the stairs to see the heater with three feet of flames coming off it. Thank goodness Patrick was only a yell away.

To keep Adam's little inquiring mind busy, his dad staked a small minibike to the ground. He gave him a small tool chest full of tools and said, "Here, tear it up." It kept Adam busy for quite a while.

Adam's next love soon became fishing. We took him to a lake and his dad was showing him how to cast the line when he looked down and saw his first fish. He dropped the fishing pole behind him and ran into the water to catch it with his bare hands. After that, I applied each year for my fishing license, and the two of us would go fishing many times in the years to follow. It was our "thing."

It took me five years to finally leave this mess. It had gotten to where Patrick went to bed angry and upset and woke up every morning even more angry. By then, I had no feelings left for this man. The anger became mental cruelty. He was never mean to Adam. Adam was all he lived for; in the end, he certainly wasn't living for me. Against my better judgment, I allowed Patrick to keep our son at the farm when I left. I felt that I could not fight with Patrick and his entire family over our boy, and I knew that he would be well taken care of by Patrick's mother.

His mother was a wonderful woman, and I loved her very much. She was happy regardless of what her husband or sons did or said to her. She was the mother of six sons. And the two that worked the farm were very disrespectful. All she wanted was for everyone to get along, but sadly, that never happened. There was never a dispute between the two of us. We always found something to laugh about. She knew our marriage was not good and that I was not happy watching all the fighting. I absorbed the pressure of it all. I knew when I left that my life would be miserable without my son. I knew leaving the family would make me one of the saddest people I had ever known, and I was right. It was a very hard transition leaving my little son behind. He was almost three when I left the farm.

Although I was to have Adam every other weekend, I was only allowed to pick him up on Friday nights at 6:00 p.m., and I was to have him back on Saturday night by 6:00 p.m. It was when he was about eight years old that I finally said, enough is enough. I became more aggressive about my rights with my son. Up till then I had been scared to death of Patrick's anger. He was afraid that I would try to take his son away from him. He told me I would never have to pay child support, but shortly after our divorce I was ordered to pay forty-five dollars a week to Patrick, and I believe it was called Child Support. To make matters worse, I was only the second woman in my county to have to pay child support in the early eighties.

It was cold and sad during those years. I was determined to make my little home the best I could for Christina. It was a challenge trying to provide as much time with her and her little brother as possible. Times were hard as I tried to work minimum--wage jobs. Larry and Bonnie Ulrey shared a great deal of love with me, and they were always there to pick up the pieces and try to help me with little bills. Bonnie made sure both of my children had new school clothes at the beginning of each school year. I could not have made it through without their unconditional love and generosity.

Soon after I divorced Patrick, I accepted an opportunity to become a basic Emergency Medical Technician. Christina, at the age of eight, accompanied me to the required classes and brushed the manikins' hair during our classes. I had always wanted to be an emergency medical technician (EMT). I wanted to understand what had really happened to my mother the night they took her away for the final time. I asked many questions during these classes, and some of the mysteries that had gnawed at me for so many years were solved. During my tenure of eight years as an EMT volunteer, I met hundreds of great people and even became a CPR/First Aid instructor. This was such a positive direction for my life. I thoroughly enjoyed helping people; it was so rewarding for me to assist on life-saving efforts and realize I was making a difference.

One Easter, when Adam was five, I was talking to my ex-mother-in-law on the phone. We were making plans for me to pick my son up for a visit. My wonderful ex-mother–in-law served as a go-between in planning my visits with my son for the first five years after my divorce. Several times after I had left the farm, I had gone to visit, and I would take her blood pressure to help her monitor it. Sometimes she would ask me to come out just to visit. We had always gotten along well together. Once she even made a statement about her son that I'll never forget. She said that she didn't know how I lived with him for six years—she couldn't have done it for one! We always laughed about the men in that family and their tempers. In spite of how well I got along with my in-laws, it still hurt, because I felt that they had done their best to hide this side of things until I was married into the family.

We had been on the phone for about fifteen minutes that day, when I suddenly noticed that her speech was slurring. I instantly went into EMT mode and asked her if she was okay. She said she was and that she was going to hang up and lie down to take a nap. I could hear Adam's voice in the background, which was comforting to me. Adam usually stayed with her during the day when the men were in the fields working. I knew he was always with a happy lady—she had such a comforting laugh. My life felt so out of control not having my baby with me, but I knew he was happy with his grandma and grandpa.

We hung up, and about ten minutes later my pager went off, displaying the farm's address. Somehow I knew my ex-mother-in-law was in trouble. I raced down to the squad house. I knew the drive from Fredericktown to the family farm took about twenty minutes. I knew from the way she had last spoken on the phone, if it really was her we were going for, that we wouldn't get there in time. I was very new with this department, and they did not know I was related to the family. If they had known, I would not have been allowed to go on this run. I pulled the ambulance out and had the door down before any of the other members arrived. My partner, who drove, was confused on the directions. I told him to go ahead and roll the squad—that I knew right where we were going and it was about a twenty-minute drive. I desperately wanted to say that my son was at the same house, but I kept these thoughts to myself, because they would not have let me go if they had known.

The man driving had a personality that most would not want to work with, and I always got stuck with him. The drive was anything but pleasant. He was certainly not a pleasant person. The farm was out in the middle of nowhere, and the guy driving kept looking at me as if I were crazy. He was convinced that I had him lost. When we arrived, one of the town's policemen, who was also an EMT, was already there, filling out a report. He pointed to me and told me to go over and check for vital signs. I knew what he wanted me to do, and pronouncing dead the most wonderful lady in my life was not what I had envisioned when I'd decided to go on this run. As I looked over and saw her lying on the couch, motionless, I looked back at him and said, "Please, not me. Let someone else do it." He motioned to me again to go over and listen for sounds of life. I again asked him to please not let it be me that pronounced her dead.

By this time, all I wanted to do was run outside and throw up. The steps I took toward this wonderful lady became the slowest steps of my life. I was twelve feet away from her. My son was nowhere around. I remember falling on my knees before her and wanting so much to pick her up and hold her, but I couldn't. I couldn't let the others know my connection with her. She was still warm but obviously had no signs of life. The smell of her perfume still fills my memory. I hung onto my memories of her to make it through the next few moments.

I went to the kitchen, where the policeman was making out the report, and told him there were no signs of life. He continued to ask my ex-father-in-law the standard questions; it was then that he asked him for the phone number to the house. He looked right at me, pointed, and said, "Ask that bitch—she was the one who called and killed her." I started shaking uncontrollably. At this point, the others looked at me and managed to put the whole picture together, guessing that we were related. I was ordered to the front seat of the squad.

The words that I had "killed her" kept echoing through my head. We were given orders to take her straight to the funeral home. She had not wanted an autopsy, and her doctor was the county coroner, so he was able to honor her wishes, which made me feel better. I knew there was a chance that I might get a quiet moment alone with her before we left. The funeral director agreed, with some hesitation, but they left me alone with her. It was hard to see her on the cold steel table. I remember she was still warm and smelled so good. She always wore perfume that lit up a room. I held her hand, knowing this would be the last time I saw her, and I prayed that she would rest in peace.

She had been ill for quite some time. I knew that mourning this wonderful lady would be easier for me because I knew she was gone. I had never had that opportunity to see my own mother after her death, which had caused doubt and bad dreams for years to come. I was told that the funeral home had been given strict instructions not to let me into the parlor to pay my respects to my mother-in-law. I didn't even try to go. After the accusation that I had killed her, I was not going near any of them. What a horrible thing to accuse me of, just because I had the last conversation with her before she died. The rumor in the neighborhood was that I had upset her on the phone, causing her death. I knew differently.

Between the losses of my own mother all those years ago, and now this wonderful lady, my heart was broken. She had told me that I had always respected her and that I was the one who had pulled her through the death of her own mother, Alice, only two years before. My son, Adam, came to me a year after his grandma had died and asked me, "Mommy, why did you kill my grandma?" His daddy had told him that his mommy had killed his grandma. The pain turned instantly into an anger that nagged at me for years. Now they had brought my little boy into this vicious mess! Again, at the age of twenty-six, I asked myself why these things kept happening to me. They just never seemed to end. *Why?* What was it about me?

When I was twenty-seven, three years after I had left the farm, I was introduced to a man who would soon be my new husband. He was six feet two inches tall, with blond hair and the most beautiful blue eyes. He was a gentle soul, always peaceful and kind. This would be husband number three. I was amazed to find out he had attended the Mount Vernon Bible College during the same time I had, eleven years earlier. He had been a college student studying to be a Christian pastor. I had met him when I was sixteen, always admired him, but respected the fact that he was happily married. Now, eleven years later, we met again when I was twenty-seven years old. We were both single and very lonely. When we realized we had this time period in common, we talked for endless hours about our spiritual lives. We each shared stories about our painful experiences. He told me about how real God was to him, and how he prayed every day, and how he had left the Bible College when it closed. He told me, "I have never lost my relationship with God and my prayer life." I counted on him being my spiritual and peaceful family leader. He told me once that he hoped I would never change, because he liked me just the way I was.

The night of my tenth high-school reunion, four months later, he asked me to marry him and took me out and bought me a beautiful diamond. We met in April and were married in October that same year. We received premarital counseling from Bonnie and Larry's pastor at the Nazarene Church. Everything seemed to be normal. Two weeks after our wedding ceremony, I asked if we would be attending the same church for services on Sunday. His answer was more than a nightmare and profoundly changed my whole outlook on this new marriage. He said that we would never attend a service in a Christian church and that Christianity "repulsed" him and he would never attend a Christian service again. He told me the Christian Church embarrassed him. It was as if someone had picked up the last hope of my life for peace and dropped it off a cliff! I asked him if he was joking, and he gave me a look that put chills down my spine.

There were no explanations; that was the end of the conversation. This revelation left me stunned for quite a long time. His plan was to convert me over to Eastern philosophy. I had no idea of this plan until two weeks after we were married. I knew before we married that he had different ideas of belief, and our agreement had been that he believed his way and I believed mine. It had been an agreement. He began to try to share different tapes and books about many different types of beliefs. I had no desire to embrace his ideas. The God I knew had pulled me through blood, sweat, and tears. I knew my God. I could not believe he really wanted to change me so quickly. He made me feel I was more than broken. It was a nightmare. When I refused to read his books or listen to his tapes, he called me shallow-minded. The wheels were set in motion, and I dug my heels into the ground. I became a very angry person.

I refused to change what I knew was my salvation, and the God I knew, just to please my husband. The saddest part about his thoughts on Eastern religion was that he picked pieces from different books and had his own way of believing. My daughter, at the age of fourteen, said one day that he made up his own little religion. He could never quite tell me exactly what it was, or what he actually believed, out of all of his readings. All I knew was that it was not what I thought I had married into. It was sometimes confusing and bewildering. Early on, I found myself feeling very deceived. Later, he admitted that he had deceived me, but he still remained on a crusade to convert me to whatever it was he believed. My life pivoted daily between being a hurt little girl to being a very defensive wildcat. I stayed on constant alert to intercept whatever he might try to do to change my mind. I did pick up the books and read where his bookmarks were, to see if I could actually wrap my mind around all the different ways of beliefs. It never worked for me.

Looking back, I see I should have talked to him more about what I did read, but I was not strong enough to let that last guard down. My whole family loved him. Most of the time, I felt that they liked him more than they did me. He had a way of convincing them he was my savior; he would take care of me and fix me. Everyone loved him so much they just did not see the web of deception and manipulation that I felt was spinning out of control. He loved my kids and they loved him. During all the years we were together, I could depend on him on a daily basis to be a devoted stepdad and to be very accepting of my children, which at the time was more important than him accepting me. He had a way of making me feel physically safe but emotionally abused.

All involved were happy with our decision to be married. Both of my kids participated in the sports he was involved in. He had a way of helping them become more self-confident. He was so animated and could communicate with them on a level I could not. I have always looked back with a smile when it came to him being the perfect stepdad. I dug my heels in and finally determined that I was not broken and he did not need to fix me. This made me totally untouchable to anyone.

He told me that if I would just read *this*, or do *that*, I would be okay. It became a world of confusion. I had to stay alert, because he would try relentlessly to get me to let my guard down and accept his newfound truth or religion. Whatever he decided for the day was his belief, I never did accept it. I refused to read his books, listen to his tapes or, by this time, even listen to him. He tested me continually to see if I was becoming weak. The words *shallow-minded* came up constantly, because I wouldn't buckle.

By this time, I was at the weakest point in my life. Being dead would not even have been peaceful enough. The God that had helped that little girl in me survive would not leave me. I developed more fear of rejection, but I realized we were going in opposite directions. Moreover, he would tell me how disappointed he was that our marriage was not quite what he had hoped it would be, and that he knew we were moving in opposite directions. I believe the hurt little girl in me finally became a total rebel, and no one could touch me then. I wanted to run, but I could not fail once more. I was determined to make this marriage work. I told myself that if I did not buckle, he would come back to believing in the God I had thought we had in common. I was totally in love with someone I thought I knew, and I was a wife that he thought he could heal and mold into what his world wanted.

All of the common beliefs and conversations that had brought us together would soon tear us apart. He did not see how this was destroying me and constantly putting me on alert to see what the next plan of attack to change me would be. In my mind it got worse and worse all the time. It always brought back the memory of Dave telling everyone that I was the only child he knew that would try to put a square into a circle, and it stung like acid being thrown into my eyes. I became someone even I did not like to be with. I told myself that as long as he did not try to get to me through my kids I could handle it. He was always kind about his attempts, but it always jerked me like a rope tightening around my neck. He never saw this.

In his mind, his crusade was to just fix the hurt and injured little girl in me and make me just like him. His intent was not to be hurtful, but we both became so resistant to each other that it was not a good scene for anyone to witness—especially my daughter. At the time, I was anything but healed from the past experiences.

Without realizing it, I was now fighting ghosts from past childhood trauma as well as three major relationship failures. Being reminded often that we were going in opposite directions hurt to the core. I was madly in love with this man but could not handle the wide divide that was our marriage. I believe the end came when I asked him one day if he had ever had the kind of intimacy that he tried so hard to find in our marriage and could not. He had warned me when I first met him that if I asked a question to prepare myself for the truth, no matter how painful it was. I wanted to know exactly what it was I was lacking in this marriage.

His answer was quick, and I knew from his answer that I was fighting a losing battle. He actually yearned for me to be like another woman he had been in love with before me. It was a few days later that I sought an attorney for dissolution. Twenty-eight days later we drove to a courthouse out of town to end this marriage. We talked openly all the way there and all the way home. I got out of his car and drove off, in a pain I will never be able to describe.

We met in April 1989, married in October of 1989, and ended it in September of 1994. He soon remarried a soul friend from the past, who did have his common beliefs, and there has always been a smile in my heart that he was finally happy and had all that he longed for. The saddest part of it all was that he also divorced my children, who loved him dearly. He chose to have no contact with them after our divorce. Part of me has been sad, through the years, when they invited him to their happy moments, graduations and weddings, and he never showed up. I know in their hearts they still think happy, warm thoughts of him from time to time.

Chapter 11
Loss of an Angel

Bonnie Ulrey 1977

When I was thirty-four, Bonnie called me to come home to the farm for a visit. She asked if I wanted my prayer journal that she had kept all those years. I told her I did not think I could relive all the pain it contained. We decided to get together and hold a ceremony of sorts, to burn the journal and pray. As Bonnie lit the fire, my prayer was for God to erase all the pain we both remembered. I was completely aware that she had suffered with me through everything during those teen years. As the prayer journal went up in smoke, we both cried, knowing the healing had begun for both of us. I thanked her for being so patient and loving with me all these years.

Later that year, Bonnie called me to come out again. She told me she had just come from the hospital after having x-rays taken, because they had found a tumor in her colon area. She was a very modest person and this was such a sensitive subject for her to be discussing. The doctor did not think it was serious, but she and Larry had decided to see a specialist for a second opinion. Even though I could see on her face that she was concerned, she still tried to reassure me. The day of the second doctor's appointment, when I had not heard from Larry or Bonnie all day, I called my sister Linda (daughter number one), and I knew immediately from the sound of her voice that the news was not good.

Linda had been crying and told me that when the specialist had pulled the x-rays out of the folder he had looked at Bonnie and said, "Oh, I see you are a cancer patient." Both Bonnie and Larry were absolutely shocked! The family doctor had known it was cancer but did not want to be the one to tell them, and the specialist thought they already knew. After almost fifty years of marriage, their lives were rocked by this devastating news.

The first surgery was to remove the tumor, and I stayed with her that night in the hospital. She cried out all night in pain. She squeezed my hand as we prayed out loud, and I prayed silently. Many times over the next months she buried her face into my stomach and cried, "Why did God let this happen?"

I did not have the answers. She was my mentor and such a wonderful guardian angel. Why was this happening to her? I didn't have any answer for her except to say, "Bonnie, I don't know. God would not have let this happen if He did not think you were strong enough to handle it."

She would say, "Paula, you are right. I just wish I knew what I did to deserve this."

After she returned home, the whole family got into a routine; each knew what Bonnie needed. Each time we were able to be with her when she needed us the most. We all cherished each new day she was with us, and we still enjoyed quality time with her.

Larry learned how to care for her chemo port and tended to her so lovingly. At times I would step back and realize that one of the most beautiful love stories was unfolding before my eyes. It was the true meaning of the word *cherish*—which most of us never experience. I went with her and Larry to many doctor visits. When she became really bad, Larry would call and ask me to bring my car, because she had asked to go back to the hospital. Each visit to the hospital seemed so cruel to me. Her suffering was terrible to watch. I was constantly observing everything the hospital staff did, a few times catching some of their errors and pointing them out. Each time I was asked to accompany her, my wish for her was to be assured that she was getting the best care she could possibly have.

She would talk to me for hours about my marriage, which during this time had not yet ended but was more than on the rocks. She would say, "Just hang in there; it will get better. You cannot walk away from this one. Just live the way you know you should. Things will be okay." They did not get better.

We also talked about things that had happened when I was young, things she wanted very much to understand. We often talked about finding where Dave had moved the twins, because she was convinced that by finding them I would be able to heal in my heart. She spoke often of her prayers for them, even though she had never met them. She prayed for their safety as well. In her infinite wisdom, Bonnie had a way of knowing from her prayers that things would happen. After being with her and seeing her prayers being answered time and again, I came to believe that the twins would come into our lives again.

It was about this time that Bonnie asked me if I was ever going to tell her the whole story. She was so intent on hearing it from me in order. I was shocked that at this painful and sad time in her life she would even want to hear this story. She advised me that she would help me tell the story to many people in my future. My marriage was crumbling, and now I was away from my husband for days at a time, caring for Bonnie. But at that point I did not care about my marriage and certainly did not miss the games he played. I asked Bonnie if she wanted me to stay with her after she left the hospital, but as usual, her concern was for me, my job, and my marriage. I assured her my job was not in jeopardy for taking care of her; in fact, they approved. And for my marriage, well, her health was far more important to me right now.

In September she took a turn for the worse. By now Bonnie had heard the entire story from my eyes, and all along she had been advising me of parts I should leave out when it was time to tell it. She was convinced that God would use this story to guide others like her and Larry in their mission to help youth. She called me out to the farm on a Friday to tell me she had finished her part of the story after hearing it from me.

We went over it that Friday afternoon, along with the parts that she would never tell. Bonnie was weak, but she was strong in her affirmation that, if this story was to go out to the world, there were parts that we had to leave out. We agreed on the parts that should never be written or told, and to this day, they have never been spoken or written.

The cancer had spread to her liver and kidneys, and other organs had begun to shut down. The doctors wanted to admit her into a hospice for her last days, but Bonnie wanted to go home. Larry honored her wishes, and he and all of her children stayed at her bedside. I assured her I would not leave, and she smiled.

Larry and I stayed awake for the next three nights and days, injecting pain meds every thirty minutes to keep her comfortable. All four of her biological children stayed as near as they could in the house during this time. Her original wish had been not to have the drugs, but in the end there was no choice. She needed them for the pain. I remember her dark little eyes looking up at me when I told her we were going to be giving her the first dose.

I was an EMT, but I was not trained for hospice duty. I did it anyway, because Bonnie and Larry asked me to, not wanting a stranger involved. This would be too sacred and intimate to have a non-family member participate. It was eight days later that Bonnie took her final breath just as her daughter was walking out of the room. I stopped her and had her come back to her mother's side. I was unprepared for the family's reaction to her death./The room went from dark and quiet to an outbreak of emotion. Larry came into the room, *picking* up his bride of nearly fifty years, rocking her gently back and forth while he said a prayer over her.

The tears still pour out of me when I close my eyes and remember the sorrow and loss of losing the most special mother I had ever known. I watched her adoring husband and four children accept her loss only seven months after diagnosis.

Bonnie still lives in Larry's heart, eighteen years later, and she will always be alive in the hearts of the people that she touched. I still get condolences from people who still miss her. It was so hard watching a woman die who was more of a mom to me than my real mom. Bonnie Ulrey was a mom and friend to whomever she came in contact with. She never knew a stranger. Her greatest joy was being a total woman to her husband and *all* of her children. There will never be another Bonnie Ulrey. Her motto was always: Blossom where you are planted.

Chapter 12
Picking up the Pieces

After the funeral, I returned home to my husband. I knew there had been a woman in his life before me, with whom he had had an intimate and spiritual life. But I also suspected the two of them saw each other in more than a professional way during our marriage. They called it a professional relationship, but I knew better. He really wanted me to be like her. I knew from various people that they saw quite a bit of each other during the last couple of years of our marriage. We divorced the September following Bonnie's death, and he married this other woman very soon afterward.

After this divorce, I bought a beautiful mobile home in Mount Vernon. This was the place my daughter, who only had two years left of school, could call home—our home. Within a short amount of time, my personal walls crumbled. It was about six months later when I woke up one morning, went into my daughter's room, and said, "Christina, I am in trouble." Waking that morning had been different from any other morning I had known. I had simply not wanted to wake up and could not put one foot in front of the other. I just wanted to go to sleep. Whatever I said after that, or just the look on my face, made her understand that something was very wrong.

Not being educated on post-traumatic childhood stress, I didn't see these unchecked symptoms slipping into my adult life. I was in trouble, but I did not know the severity of what this post-traumatic childhood stress could do to me, since most of the trauma was so deep within me. It was, however, apparent to my young daughter that her mother was in big trouble.

Without a driver's license, and only a learners permit, Christina drove me to an out-of-town doctor. I believe I was finally having a full-fledged breakdown. Whatever this was, it certainly caught the attention of my two sisters. They had not been around much, because they were busy with their own lives. They had never been there for me before when I needed them, but now, all of a sudden, they wanted to help me. We all lived very far apart, but now they wanted to be near me. While both of them were in sound marriages, I was a mess and more than they could handle. I spent the next year on antidepressants and in counseling. I missed three months of work, got behind on all my bills, and did not care about anything for the first time in my life. It felt as if the doctor's main motivation was to get me addicted to drugs, but thank God, I still had the sense to know it. I did not go anywhere or talk to anyone; I was just numb.

My little girl had become my caretaker. She nursed me back to health and kicked me in the butt when I needed it. She became my rock until I threw away all the drugs I had been prescribed. Then, with help from councilors educating me on what was happening to me, and why, I was able to get a handle on my life and recognize when this post-traumatic ghost was lurking around the corner at me.

We who are survivors of this traumatic childhood stress all need education at an early age on the subject, and we need to recognize our old triggers and to understand how the stress relates to our adult lives. I believe we could head off a bunch of life issues if we had this knowledge as young folks about to launch into the real world. I believe it's as important as reading, writing, and arithmetic. With the help of education on this subject, along with some counseling, things were slowly, but surely, getting better for me. Having two children of my own, and still not understanding what was lurking in my shadows, it was a very slow walk for me to understanding.

My son was in and out of my life. He now was a preteen, getting into his own situations with his dad while still living on the farm. His visits with me became fewer and fewer, as his Boy Scouts and hunting became priorities. He became a very good hunter and was very proud to tell me of his latest hunt. Our conversations for the most part were limited to his hobbies and activities, because I was not always sure just what to talk about. His father and I still did not communicate. It would be many more years before his father and I could even speak civilly to one another.

By Christmastime I was feeling much better. My sister Sharon called me from Atlanta and asked if I was sitting down, because she was going to give me my Christmas present over the phone. After sixteen years of not seeing the twins, she had located one of them, Debbie, who was living in Texas. She gave me her phone number, saying, "Merry Christmas! Call her!"

When the shock wore off, I called my little sister Debbie. She was now a woman of twenty-seven. The last time I had seen her, she had been a child of nine. Sixteen years later, for hours and hours, we cried long-distance tears that took my phone bill out the roof. I saved money over the next year to buy Debbie's airline ticket to Mount Vernon. My boss was so excited for me that he gave me the whole week off to get to know her again. I was extremely excited about Debbie's visit, and my other two sisters were coming as well. At least four of us would all be together, finally. I was so excited that I blurted out that we should go and see Mama's grave.

As a surprise, one of my sisters had contacted Christina, to have her go to the cemetery and see if she could locate my mother's grave. I knew there would be many questions about our mother. My daughter knew that I was bringing my sisters home for a visit, so she went to the graveyard and did her own research to find my mother's gravesite. She came to me and told me she wanted to take me somewhere. I was not sure what she was doing or where we were going, but I agreed. On our way she said, "Mom, I am taking you to see your mother's gravesite. I went yesterday, and the lady walked me to the gravesite. I am taking you to see it today."

At nineteen, my own daughter was taking me to see my mother's gravesite for the first time. I wanted to just sob, and I knew, as strong as she was trying to be, that I could not let her see what my insides were doing. I felt my legs get weak knowing how many times I had walked that graveyard looking for this site. Now, at the age of thirty-five I would finally have peace. It was a very emotionally moving moment. This was a moment that no mother should have to experience in front of her daughter. I had never had this conversation with Christina. I knew, without asking her, how she had discovered the story of the unfound gravesite. She had listened to phone calls and conversations with my friend Sherri along the way, and she knew that it was a huge burden for me to find this gravesite.

Christina drove into the graveyard and parked beside the site. It was about one hundred yards from the front door of the management office. She walked over and pointed to the grave. It was unmarked, but she was sure it was the one. Everything was moving in slow motion for me. I felt the little girl emerging from me once again, even as I was standing right beside my own little girl. I was excited that this grave I had been searching out for years had finally been found. A visual came upon me, as I stood there gazing down at the site I had looked for my whole teenage years—I saw all five of us sisters gleefully dancing around the unmarked gravesite. I took note that it was located right next to the site of Baby Gump.

Since I was going to be bringing two of my sisters to the gravesite the next week, when Debbie was in town, I picked out some colorful flowers at a greenhouse and planted them there to spruce up her plot. It had no stone, only a plate in the ground bearing a number. I looked at the plate and talked to her. I remembered how I had hidden in the closet at Grandma's house after the urn was delivered, and talking to the box that sat on the shelf. I had felt safe knowing she was there, in some form. As much as I had hated Dave for not burying her, I had been glad she was still with me in that closet. My kids had never known any of this while they were growing up, nor did I want them to. It was my naiveté showing, thinking I had shielded them from knowing about my awful childhood—especially since Adam was born into the new cyberkid generation; he had read excerpts from this transcript but did not tell me for many years.

There was still much turmoil in my life and trying to find answers to still so many unanswered questions. My son was now fifteen years old, and he came to me to ask if he could live with me. He said he knew that all the horrible things his dad had told him about me were lies, and he was ready to come live with me. If there was ever an occasion to hold a party, it was this day. I thought I was dreaming, and I asked him point blank, "Adam, are you sure? And if you are not, please do not play with my heart!"

He answered, "Mom, I want to live with you and get to know you better—please say yes!" His words still cling to my heart. My strong son stood five foot nine inches tall, with dark, wavy hair, and a gentle face. I believe it would have killed him if I had said no.

Adam has a very deep heart in him. He has never talked much, but like his sister, when he did say something, you knew he had thought about it for days. I was shocked and happy all in the same moment. I asked him if I could have his permission to call his dad and talk to him about this, and he agreed. I knew then that he was serious; since he knew the relationship his father and I had was very tense and stressed. Adam would have never wanted the conflict because of himself.

When he moved in, it was strange at first, but we got along well. By now his sister was out on her own, at the age of nineteen, and living with her boyfriend of three years. We lived through his "Casanova" days with the girls, and while there were some trying times, for the most part he was very respectful of me. His heart has always been strong and loyal, and since his only request was that I get along with his father, I made sure that Patrick and I never had cross words from that day forward.

Now it was finally time to meet Debbie at the airport. When I arrived there to meet my sister, my stomach was in knots with apprehension. I expected to see the same little girl who had run out of the garage and handed me the mirror. But when she stepped out of the airport tunnel, she was a grown woman, with her own child in her arms, two-year-old Nicholas. I went to hug her, and she put her arm out to keep me from getting close. I felt horrible. I could see that the years had made her hard. It didn't matter—she was here now. Bonnie had been right; we would find them again. I closed my eyes and said, "Wherever you are, Bonnie, I know you have to be smiling right now. Thank you a thousand times."

We asked so many questions of each other. She asked about Mama, things like: What color hair did she have? What color eyes? Was she short, fat, tall, skinny? Who was she? After she asked all of her questions, I had to start asking mine. My burning questions were: Did our stepmother ever quit beating you? and How did you get to Dallas? The stories that she shared were heart-wrenching. We three oldest sisters had escaped within an inch of our lives. The other twin, Deon, remains under doctor's care most of the time, sometimes in a lock-down facility. She still lives near or with Dave and Lynn.

Debbie got shipped to Texas when she was fifteen, after she drew back and hit Lynn in the mouth in retaliation. Dave almost broke her arm, and he sent her away to Texas to live with Lynn's daughter. Debbie described herself as a "drug-addicted survivor" after being sent to Texas. Dave and Lynn were called to her hospital bed numerous times. I believe what finally pulled her through were the daily devotions and prayers coming from Bonnie. Debbie is a strong woman with a heart of gold. She has three sons and a daughter, and I've been fortunate to be able to fly to visit her in Dallas, Texas, three times. She still cries when she relives the nightmares, but she is healing, as we all are. When she needs advice, she calls me, her "big sis." We still cry tears when we speak, and each time we speak of the past, a piece is cleared away.

When we three older sisters get together as adults, we have learned, two of us can make it for a short time with no explosions—but put three of us together, and watch out! We are like charged dynamite; some kind of explosion is guaranteed to happen, even though we never know what will trigger the next blast. My children noticed it long before we did. My children did not feel comfortable being around us as a group of three.

If I could tell caseworkers and counselors anything about siblings being torn apart, I would tell them that I know from my speaking and research that sometimes siblings have to be split. There are situations in which it can't be helped. Sibling separation happens all over the world, due to many things, not just trauma. I believe it is more critical to set up visitation or phone calls from day one and not let the child down when he or she is waiting anxiously to see or hear from siblings. As the eldest of five sisters, I regret that from the beginning of our separation—due to the lie Dave told when he surrendered us—we could not visit or call each other for a whole year. That lie prompted a whole year of investigation, one that we did not understand.

We had no chance for phone calls or visitations, which I believe actually did us more harm than being separated. For me, this caused the lurking monster that emerges from post-traumatic childhood stress. If that were not bad enough, the authorities, with no warning, decided to reunite siblings who had already grieved each other as dead. Everyone thinks it's a wondrous celebration—but the siblings were left numb and unable to figure out how to reconnect. Experiencing as the oldest sister what everyone thought would be the best thing that had ever happened to us—two sisters being reunited—I can tell you that this was daunting! Today, as we look back and still try so hard to be loving sisters, we have discussed the fact that we could have healed and reconnected much easier with the help of counseling.

If there were no funds for counseling, maybe at our teenage years we could have used education on what this experience of being separated and reconnected could do and how to recognize triggers. I am sure that anyone reading this story who has experienced anything similar knows what *triggers* are. If you are interested in learning more, please research post-traumatic childhood stress.

As for me, reading as much as I can has given me such an understanding and even allowed me to recognize the moments when I need to just take care of myself. In the seventies, the child-care agencies were not as informed on this condition and what the long-term effects could be on an adult's life if it were not recognized. They did not offer services, because it was not quite understood yet. Today you can google this on your computer and begin to help yourself. You can read and understand what triggers are lurking in your life and then act on changing them. My two sisters and I suffered a double whammy. Not only were we separated, we did not have the ability to call and visit for the first year. Worse, the agencies were not aware of the devastation this would cause in our adult lives as sisters. This has put a strain on our adult relationships, both with our sisters and with other adults. There was damage done to us that could have been avoided with today's education and information. It is my hope that no one goes their whole life living in this post-traumatic dysfunctional life without seeking some sort of help.

Chapter 13
Paula's Reflections

Paula – 2011 Pondering the memoir journey

At the age of fifty, I ponder the moments and events that happened along the way, and I recognize the influential people who contributed to my happiness and sanity. These are the people that prevented me from becoming that twelve-year-old broken child that the counselor pegged me for, the one that should have ended up in a straightjacket, locked away in a rubber room.

The most recent studies show that sibling relationships are potentially the longest relationships we will ever make. Mental health professionals have recently placed more recognition on their significance, and some even believe that they are more influential than the relationships with our parents, spouses, and even our own children. These studies do not surprise me; I felt as if I were going mad during different phases of my life without my siblings.

After going in and out of six other homes in that first year, I remember as if it were yesterday that day in December of 1975, shortly before I turned fourteen, when I was invited to become part of Larry and Bonnie Ulrey's family. Though this journey of six new homes was not the painful part. The painful part was being part of a family of five sisters and a step brother two years older; it was our separation. Before meeting this unique, loving, and committed Ulrey family, I felt as if I had been bleeding for that whole year. I was quite detached and somewhat numb to life. I was alone, scared, and wondering when the next change or new home was coming. I was, to put it simply, a complete mess. From October 1974 to December 1975, the unique challenges of seven different foster homes had systematically destroyed all of my coping mechanisms—the essential skills that most teens automatically possess. What profound, wonderful people Larry and Bonnie Ulrey were in my life!

Another opportunity that I know changed my life and helped me hold on was when Judith Goodhand, another very profound woman in my life, requested that I participate in the prospective foster-parenting training videos and panels. This opportunity helped me tremendously in coping. The panel was simply a group of prospective foster parents asking me some personal, and sometimes invasive, questions about my foster-care experience. The most important thing regarding that experience was that I was advised that I always had a choice. I could answer the question, or choose not to, if it was too hard. *Choices* helped build that lost self-esteem; they were a huge building block of sorts. I would answer as openly as possible. It allowed me to get the reassurance that my life events should not have happened to me or to any child. I received praise. These experiences made me feel, for the first time, respected for my courage—sometimes with hugs, sometimes laughter, and sometimes tears. Judith gave me permission to feel whatever I needed to.

During one of my last panel meetings as a foster child, my new dad, Larry, wrote a poem about me that Judith stood and read to the group. After she read it, my very special dad, Larry, stood up and clapped as loudly as he could, as if to praise me in front of all the new parents waiting to experience their first foster children. What a feeling that was! There was not a dry eye in the room.

My two main goals in life became to reunite all my sisters and become one big happy family, and to locate my mother's grave and have a funeral for her. The goal of bringing my family back together became a huge obsession and somewhat out of control at points in my life. Both these plans made me absolutely crazy at times. I just could not make it work out. In my mind, I was never a complete mother, daughter, employee, friend, or especially, sister because of this. Staying focused on anything except finding a way to make these things happen became daunting.

I did manage to locate all of my sisters. I have never been able to bring all five of us together in the same room—yet. I have accepted that we are a divided sisterhood, and I am grateful that I at least have relationships with all of them separately. I love each of them, and I wish them well in their individual lives. I have let go of my obsession. The realization of short visits with one or two at a time is a reality and works quite well. Even within great families, short visits are always best at times—so it is with my two sisters and I.

The twins exist in a whole different world, one of which we did not get the privilege to be a part. The twins will occasionally check in to share their current life stories. They are often very sad and full of devastation and crisis to the full extreme. I often leave these conversations not knowing how to feel or think. All I can do at this time is send a few dollars and pray for their protection.

The story of mother's gravesite is a convoluted and very confusing one. There was a time when I thought my daughter had found the site where she rested. In the beginning, I would visit the site or plant flowers. Then new stories arose that Mama really was not buried there after all. Apparently, the cemetery office paperwork was in question. To get more information, I went to a family member of Dave's. This person had it on good authority that

Mama was buried somewhere in the yard of the house where we'd lived, where we were separated when I was twelve. Apparently Dave knew I was searching for my mother's remains or gravesite. He came back to Mount Vernon in July of 2007 to place a stone on the gravesite, finally, thirty-five years after her death.

This still did not explain why there was no receipt on record for the burial. After hours of looking and researching with the office manager at the cemetery office for the receipt of burial, we could not find it. The purchasing of the baby lot for fifteen dollars was on record, but there was no receipt for the opening and closing of the gravesite. My mother's plot was the only one in the office that did not have the second receipt!

I cannot really put into words what happened to me the night that I learned this. It was a total body-and-soul shakeup. The ten-mile drive home seemed to take ten years. My anger resurfaced that he (or anyone) could do this unthinkable thing. The thought that my mother was buried in some flower garden just because he "did not know what to do with her urn that day" was insane. To this day, I do not know for sure what the truth is, and I probably never will.

My new plan was to write a eulogy and perhaps have a funeral for my mother. My plans were to share with readers some closure for this untimely death of my mother so many years ago and to bring this pain to an end. But no matter how hard I tried, I just could not bring myself to come up with the words. I could not even get on paper the first sentence. I could close my eyes and remember my mother laughing and singing with Elvis and squealing with delight when she watched him on TV. She would sing to her little girls, and I remember kisses on the cheeks, hugs as she tucked us into bed, the stories she would read, her laughter and her smell, her beautiful voice and shiny hair—but I could not find words for this eulogy.

No, I could not write the eulogy. At the age of forty-eight, I called Judith and shared my struggle with this last chapter of my memoir. This "closure" concept for my mother was driving me mad! Most people I had talked to about it said I needed to achieve closure for myself, to allow the grieving, and to accept her death once and for all.

Judith has always been wise, and having worked with children for fifty-some years, she was a woman who knew me inside and out when I was a youth under her care. She would surely have some words of wisdom that would help put this nightmare to rest. She said, "Paula, if there was anything I remember about you, when you talked to me about your mother, it was as if she were still alive and in the same room with us. Why do you want to bury her now? You have kept her alive all these years. Maybe you should think about keeping her alive in your heart and not making her memories go away." It was if her words picked me up and I confronted this miserable monster of grief and looked him right in the eye. I felt instantly energized, as if a fresh spring breeze had come over me and swept away the load I had been carrying throughout my entire adult life. Judith's inspiration allowed me to realize that I should keep my mother alive in my heart, and not mourn her death. Oh, what a happy day!

On the Edge of Unthinkable is about how my life unfolded during different phases. One of my biggest fears, which stayed with me throughout each phase, was the fear of falling off the edge and losing my sanity. After that last enlightening conversation with Judith, I was walking alone down a long corridor, when that very familiar black feeling came over me again. It was the uncertainty of how long I could hold on this time and keep myself together before I truly lost my mind. I realized then, at that moment, that I did not have to accept this sort of "fragile" thinking anymore. I made the decision that I am never going to permit myself to entertain these thoughts or let them have power over me again.

If I did, I would be giving people that had harmed me or my sisters the power to destroy the rest of my life, and I did not want or need that negative power or energy in my life. Holding my head up high, standing tall, and truly putting those thoughts safely in the past has brought me to a place in my life that I can say I am proud of.

It has been a long journey, but I am finally at rest with the story I have shared. I placed those re-taped boxes back on the shelves in my mind, and I will never open them again. With the help of many special people in my life, and burying myself into this story for the last twenty-four years, trying to make perfect sense of it, I can honestly say I finally feel healthy in mind and spirit.

Within the last thirty-eight years, the mutual respect and commitment have remained between my dad, Larry, and me. We have learned a lot from and about each other. Larry is eighty-seven years old now and still stays involved with all of his children and grandchildren. Some memories about Larry that will never leave me involve his being a pilot. He took us on many Sunday-morning flights up to Lake Erie Island for breakfast and rides around the island on golf carts. I also remember the times we flew over the Fourth of July fireworks to see all the beautiful colors. These were just some of the ways he showed all of his children all the colors of love.

Larry was the best dad in the world to me. When he made the commitment to be my new dad, he did so with a no-matter-what attitude and true commitment. That meant the world to me. I wish every child in this world could have a dad just like him. Larry never uttered the words "foster daughter" to anyone, and he allowed me to be his own "daughter number two." He showed unconditional love to me and to all the other children he committed to. If there were a blue ribbon for Best Dad in the World, it would be his, without question. Mike, Lee, Mark, and Linda shared their parents with all of us. They showed my sister Sharon and me the same unconditional love that Larry did. They have been so gracious through the years. I thank God for them, and I thank Judith Goodhand for telling Larry and Bonnie about this troubled teenager so many years ago.

Larry Ulrey – 2010 The Sunday surprise ride after breakfast

Chapter 14
The Final Reach

Foster care has come a very long way since its origination in 1945. Before this time, all the unwanted or orphaned children went to institutions or orphanages. Thousands of children died from the poorly run orphanages and illnesses that were spread amongst them. By 1950, statistics showed that children in foster care far outnumbered the children in the orphanages, with more than twice as many in foster care. By the late 1970s, the foster care population exceeded 800,000, roughly where it stands today.

Simply put, foster care is a system by which adults care for minor children who are not able to live with their biological parents. In some cases, the child has little or no chance to return to his or her parents' custody. This was the case for my sisters and me. According to the AFCARS (*Adoption and Foster Care Analysis and Reporting System*, the statistics data), today 32 percent of the children in foster care are five or under years of age, 28 percent of foster children are between six and twelve years of age, and finally, 40 percent are between the ages of thirteen and twenty-one. As you can see, the preteens and teenagers are the highest, in the range of thirteen to twenty-one.

My sisters and I fell into this category. Currently there is a shortage of foster homes for the teenagers in foster care. Statistics show that in our current economic crisis, if things do not change by the year 2020, 22,500 kids will die of abuse or neglect—most before their fifth birthday. The need for foster parents today is crucial to keep this from happening!

In 1978 I became one of the 9 percent of kids every year that age out of the foster-care system. I was emancipated at the age of seventeen to begin life on my own. The difference between me and the majority of the youth who abruptly age out of the system was that I had a child of my own before the age of eighteen. Against all odds, I graduated from high school in 1979 with my class. Larry and Bonnie knew that this was one of the most important things I needed to accomplish. With the promise I made to them, my achievement to graduate would be the most important goal to sustain my self-esteem and the desire to contribute to society. There was no way I could let them down.

Even after graduation, my body, spirit, and soul were still haunted by the scars left behind by the feelings of abandonment, and from being separated from my sisters. As you have seen, my sibling group was not the average. We were not privileged to have visitation for the first year after separation, due to Dave's terrible lie when we were surrendered.

Recent studies have proven that it is not the separation of siblings that creates the ultimate harm; it is the lack of communication and visitation that occurs. Studies also show that sibling relationships are potentially the longest relationships we will ever have. There has been more recognition of the significance of this. Some even believe that these relationships are more influential than the relationships with our parents, spouses, or children! These sibling ties can weather distance, aging, and disagreements, as well as provide great support throughout our lives.

After years of my own research and reading, it has been no surprise that being separated from my sisters had almost driven me mad. It has taken me until almost the age of fifty to come to grips with what actually happened and the role it played throughout my entire life. My siblings were out of sight—but never out of mind.

With help from committed counselors and friends, I developed a tool that proved to be very helpful to my healing process. While I was in counseling, someone suggested that I begin journaling my thoughts and feelings. I did not understand at the time what an impact this simple suggestion would have on me. We were taught to recognize panic attacks or a devastating crisis. During this time I learned to always dart for that pad of paper and pen. The writing sometimes seemed daunting. I found that this did seem to allow me to decompress and diffuse the emotional crisis.

More often than not, I could go back and review my thoughts to gain a better understanding of the triggers that had started the crisis. Reading my thoughts over again in the journal helped me link the actions to the feelings that plagued me. This is beneficial to both my well-being and my mental freedom. Believe me when I say I have a trunk of journals. Those journals are what prompted me to spend twenty-five years drafting out this memoir. There were still some times when journaling did not help, but those times were few and far between.

Lessons on what support systems are available—such as crisis hot lines and free-self help groups that I could call on—were always a huge help. Searching for these avenues was not easy; Judith and my case managers had to teach me how to seek them. I hope that as you read this now you do not wait to help yourself after you have fallen more often than you have stood up through adversity. It was always very important to me to have that one support person I could call with anything that was weighing on my mind.

When all else failed, being taught the difference between a temporary crisis and a crisis that would require a counselor was an integral part of learning, and learning how to emotionally support myself was critical. During the process of recovering from past childhood trauma, we all need to know where to sustain help in healing, before it causes us to take steps backward in our healing journey.

All of these services are available to anyone who has that survival instinct to heal and survive after adversity. Making the decision to move forward in my life, and not allow the trauma of my childhood to dictate the paths that I would take, was my first huge leap toward moving beyond the past. You have to help yourself and reach out for whatever it takes to bring yourself closer to an inner peace. Our lives are very similar to a hand of playing cards. You can simply throw it away, or you can make that choice to deal with it the best way you can.

Participating in group therapy was also very helpful to me as a young woman; one such group taught us how to become more assertive, for example. Some of these groups are even offered as a free service to adults in your communities. If you are looking for services as described above, the local Job and Family Services or Mental Health Association in your community can point you to the right paths.

While out on my own at a very early age, and being a young mother, I was encouraged to remain in associations of sorts. The Family Services Department of the county where I lived asked me to hold a weekly infant stimulation class in my home. While my little baby was growing, I was privileged to have child-care workers helping me begin this journey. We all learned so much about the growing and nurturing of babies. Each week we had a guest speaker and about twenty babies crawling around on cushioned mats while we learned the latest and greatest in child care. I conducted this little club until my baby was around one year old.

I worked most of my life either as a secretary or in marketing and sales. I was always able to achieve any goal my employers set for me. When evaluated, I always rose above standard. Larry and Bonnie taught me the basics of social and work skills and encouraged me to always be a lady and to be professional. Those lessons gave me the courage and drive to work and earn a wage to pay my bills, and to raise my children the very best I knew how.

Chapter 15
Larry Remembers

Larry Ulrey - #85 Birthday at the diner

Larry Ulrey 2010 "Yes, I think I like this"

My name is Lawrence Ulrey, and it is my great pleasure to contribute a chapter to Paula's memoir.

Bonnie and I raised four "birth" children. By 1974, each of them had grown up and was supporting him- or herself. They visited us often, but the house was quiet.

Children's Services (CS) was on a campaign encouraging couples to foster children who lived in children's homes. I was being paid more by my employer than I was worth, and Bonnie and I wanted to do something important. We decided to foster a child.

We attended the required training sessions and fulfilled the requirements. I wanted a boy. Bonnie wanted him to be at least ten. CS brought us a twelve-year-old boy. He had been in one other foster home before ours. He had an older brother, whom he talked to at school. The brother described how much fun his family was having without him, or something like that. Jim was with us for four months.

After Jim left, the director of CS, Judith Goodhand, asked Bonnie and me to meet with her. She wanted us to accept a thirteen-year-old girl. She said, "Paula tells unimaginable stories, but she never lies."

Judith added, "Paula has two younger sisters who live in separate foster homes. She is passionately determined for herself and her sisters to live together in one place. She is convinced that there exists somewhere a legal document initiated by her parents that decrees the three girls must live apart."

Bonnie and I agreed to an introduction dinner at our house, where we three could decide whether we liked or disliked each other. Paula revealed quickly that her grammar needed repair. A CS agent had brought Paula. She and the agent roamed our house and grounds after dinner. When they came back, Paula asked us if she could have a cat.

After dinner on her first permanent day with us, Paula asked if she could use the phone. I said yes. She talked from that moment until bedtime. I was more afraid of her than she was of me, but finally, I did tell her to go to bed. She argued that she just wanted to let a couple more of her friends know where she lived now. After I reminded her that she had school tomorrow, she went upstairs to bed—I thought!

Actually, she stayed in her room until she concluded I was asleep, and then she went back downstairs, put a blanket over herself and the phone, and continued telling her friends where she lived. When I caught her at it, I must have been more persuasive, because she stayed upstairs until the next morning.

Calls from boys were a small, almost fun, problem. They phoned continually, until I realized that when I answered their requests were always the same two words: "Paula there?" From then on, if Paula was home, and hadn't outraced me to the phone, I would answer yes to that query. If there were no further questions in a reasonable time, I would hang up.

I told Paula I would let a boy caller talk to her only if he told me his name, without my asking for it, and then asked, "May I speak to Paula?" I hate rules, but that procedure reduced phone call frequency at our house by at least 50 percent. (There were a few callers that did follow my prescribed format.)

In those early days, we couldn't share similar past experiences, because there weren't any. Reminding each other of our trip to

Middle Bass Island got monotonous quickly. We watched movies, Bill Cosby, etc., but beyond that we were each limited to stories that the other didn't enjoy. I hated hearing about Paula's past in army posts and so on, because I was jealous. I wished so much we could have raised her beginning on January 1, 1961.

Among later and lighter at-home matters, there arose the question of how much makeup a high school girl should wear. I said the white stuff she used made her eyes look like white side-wall tires, and I asked her, "How do you get them even, when you must close one eye to paint the other one?" She didn't answer stupid questions like those! I sure enjoyed asking them, though.

When she lived with Bonnie and me, Paula attended the same school that she had attended while living in her previous homes. Judging by grades, she was a fair student. Judging by her total neglect of study between tests, she was brilliant. Only late in the evening before a test would she study, "Just enough to pass," using her words. The teachers we met at the parent-teacher meetings liked her but usually remarked that she talked too much. As for student councilors, she outwitted them easily.

The time came for one of the larger employers in Mount Vernon, the Pittsburgh Plate Glass Company, to stop operating. PPGC offered jobs in Texas to selected Ohio employees. Paula's sister, Sharon, was a foster daughter of one of those families.

While the PPGC shutdown was still a rumor, Bonnie and Judith, with legal help, overturned the absurdity that separated the sisters—the charge that only Paula remembered. That triumph made it legal for Paula, Sharon, and Terry to live in the same household.

Not long thereafter, Bonnie prepared our house and got together some party food for a celebration. She invited our older kids to attend.

My task for the event was to pick up Sharon and have her home to our house before Paula's school bus stopped out in front. I did that, and while Paula was walking up the driveway, Sharon hid in a closet. We let Paula come in and become a bit baffled about all the people. Then, per Bonnie's plan, Sharon burst out of the closet and shouted, "Surprise!" It was a great success. Most things Bonnie did were successful.

The third sister, Terry, chose not to leave where she was. She visited and overnighted often, but she never succumbed to Paula's urgings to move in with us.

I think ours was Paula's first and only home in the country. She had learned to skate in the roller rink in Mount Vernon and, in my opinion, was expert. Forward, backward, one foot, whirl, race—you name it. She begged to go there every time it was open. It closed at 11:00 p.m. At first I would take her there, go home, and be there again to pick her up when the place closed.

Then I learned that her favorite boyfriend lived just a few blocks from the skating rink. After that I never stayed away from the rink for longer than fifteen minutes when she was there after dark. I told her to stay inside the rink. I told her "Don't go to his house; don't sit in cars," etc. I didn't have enough guts to tell her she couldn't go skating for *X* number of weeks if she disobeyed. I remember being pleased with myself after that talk. Her answers to my questions were what I thought they should be.

After her pregnancy was confirmed, we talked a bit again about our previous conversation. One of her answers was, "I didn't say I wouldn't have sex."

As Judith said, "She never lies."

Recognition of Paula's condition and a decision for abortion seemed simultaneous. CS arranged a date and location for the operation and counseled Paula continuously. Judith said Bonnie and I would not be permitted to drive Paula to the clinic, but we could drive her home, "If there are no complications in the procedure."

We waited in our car. Bonnie and I rode in the front seat and Sharon in back. Bonnie prayed for all of us, especially the abandoned one. I remember opening the car door for Paula, and Judith saying something like, "Paula is just fine; you may take her home." That incident troubled Bonnie to the end of her life.

Most girls want to own a horse, for reasons I don't understand. Linda, our number-one daughter, had owned her horse for a long time. She had named him Kit and rode him on lightly traveled roads most high school summer-vacation days and in the Knox County horse club, etc. Paula, number-two daughter, chose a horse smaller than Kit and named him Buddy. She wasn't into cruising country roads—unless maybe she could have done it all at Buddy's top speed.

On two occasions I watched Linda and Paula race. Each horse was without a saddle and each girl without shoes. The course was pretty close to a fifth of a mile long, in a field near our house. The race started next to the fence at the far side of the field. On the near end of the course there was a gravel driveway to cross before entering the backyard, and in the backyard was a concrete walk about thirty feet beyond the driveway. The driveway marked the end of the course. It's wise that I don't tell you who won either contest, but I will say that each time they crossed the driveway, the horses were neck and neck, and each horse ruined a lot of grass sliding to stop before reaching the concrete walk.

I helped daughter number-three, Sharon, select her horse. She named him Mighty. It was a poor choice—he was not a fun horse. Sharon tried hard to do some of the things that Paula did, but—I should not have kept that horse!—she was thrown, and her arm was broken. Again Bonnie took over. When I got home from work, Sharon's arm was in a sling, and she had recovered enough to be mumbling about shooting the horse and never getting on one again.

Paula learned to drive on Sunday mornings on the way home from church. Bonnie worried that the police would stop us and find Paula was too young for a license. Sharon was always frightened and sat scooted way down on the back seat. As soon as we were out on the back roads, Paula would start: "Can I drive? Can I drive?" (That was before I had finished correcting her grammar.) Paula would scoot over while I walked around to the passenger side.

I made her practice quick stops. I would assign a speed, and when there was no traffic ahead or behind, I would say, "Stop before you get to that mailbox." And I made her (when there was no traffic near) practice steering the two right-side wheels to the ditch side of the berm and back onto the pavement. Four-speed stick didn't bother her a bit.

Shortly after she got her driver's license, Paula drove some girlfriends to Coshocton and then drove all the way back in my '78 VW Vanagon with the parking brake set. She diagnosed the fault: "It runs fine but smells terrible."

On one snowy school morning, Bonnie said, "Don't let her drive to school today," but I did, and Bonnie said, "You're making a big mistake." Bonnie was correct. I came along a few minutes later, and there was my '80 Opel Kadette on its side in a field on the other side of the ditch. The two girls, Paula and Sharon, were sitting on the left door, crying.

Paula was in a third automobile incident when she was twenty-six years old. Several years after she started living on her own, she was hit head on by a Chevrolet Corvette. A drunk was at the wheel. Paula's car had to be sectioned to enable the rescue personnel to reach her and put her into braces.

We were asleep when someone from St. Ann's hospital called and ask if I was the father of Paula Kyle. After I answered yes, he said Paula was in their emergency room. He wouldn't tell me her condition, but he said the accident had been a very bad one. He urged me (us) to come there "as quickly as you can."

We arrived at St. Ann's between two and three o'clock in the morning. Somebody told us to wait where we were. A nun walked up then and said, "Your daughter is not awake right now, but I will take you up to see her when you're ready." I remember with admiration that that nun answered our most important question before we asked it. St. Ann's has been my favorite hospital ever since.

Paula was good at finding and doing jobs and then moving on to better ones. Bonnie babysat for Paula's daughter through that five-or-so-year period. Christina became a nurse who tells other nurses what to do. She wrote a chapter for this book. Be sure to read it.

You asked whether Paula recovered from the accident quickly and fully. Yes to the *quickly*. More (several years) about *fully*: she was left with a scar on her right cheek. She is proud of being a blonde with one dimple. Ask her.

I did my best to avoid being called a foster parent. For a long time I answered truthfully and said yes when asked. I hated hearing the girls being called *foster* children.

I liked it when we were asked, "Which ones are the foster children?" because then we could answer, "I forget."

Now I say, "We adopted them." I finally remembered we adopted them in our hearts. The legal stuff is in a lawyer's desk.

I welcome any and all questions about our adopted kids.

I have respect for Children's Services. They do jobs that I couldn't do and wouldn't want to do.

Bonnie did more—far more—for Paula and Sharon than I did. My input was chauffeuring, some money, and some enforced studying. Bonnie said she taught them womanly things. She made them do housework. She said, "Somebody has really taught them well about housework."

Bonnie loved the Lord. She thought every morning was the beginning of another exciting new adventure. Her motto and advice for all was: Blossom where you're planted.

Chapter 16
Christina Ann Remembers

Christina – High School graduation Party

My name is Christina Ann. I am thirty-three years old and would like to add my thoughts to my mother's book. I have never been a great supporter of "the book." I know that my mother does not understand why, and I know it hurts her. I have not read it, and I may never. It's very hard to explain the deluge of feelings that come up when I think about reading it; I don't even think that I completely understand it myself. I have shared in her pain for my entire life, and I cannot bear to live it again between the covers of a book. It kills me to think of others reading about her life for entertainment.

My mom sees the bigger picture that I cannot. She wants to use her experience to help others; she wants to make a difference in a broken system. My greatest fear is that she will not get the closure that she so badly wants, and I cannot bear to see her hurt again by the contents of this book. You have already read my mother's story; you know about the abuse, the pain, the feelings of being left alone in the world, and the great void that was created within her. I am the filler of the void—that is why I was created; that is why I am here. The love of a child is unconditional and pure, the perfect cure for a lifetime of pain. It's a heavy weight for any child to bear, filling the void in a mother's heart, being her rock. No matter what happens now, she has me. She will never be alone in the world again. When she crumbles, I am there to lift her back up. When she is in pain, I hurt, too.

I don't think that she understands this even now, how deeply her pain truly hurts me. I've always known about my mother's childhood, that she was separated from my aunts and they were sent to different foster homes. She never tried to hide these things from me; maybe that's why it has always seemed somewhat normal to me, because I never knew any different. There was never a big sit-down discussion about what happened and why; it was just always part of our life. I never felt any stigma for being the child of a foster kid; I didn't even know that there was any reason to feel different.

What I did understand, even as a small child, was that the end product of my mom being in all of those foster homes was that she came to live with my grandparents, and they loved her, and they loved me. I never once felt as though I were any different than their other grandchildren. The relationship between my mom and her sisters was troubled. When I was young I spent a lot of time with Aunt Sharon and her boys. Even as young as I was at the time, I knew that Sharon did not approve of the decisions that my mom made, no matter what the reasons were behind them. She would often tell me that she knew that someday I would end up on her doorstep and that she and her husband would take me in as their daughter.

There was always some drama between Sharon and my mom, and I was usually stuck in the middle of it all. Aunt Terry never really lived close to us after college; our relationship with her was phone calls and a few visits over the years, usually on special occasions. As a teen and an adult, I learned quickly to avoid the rare occasion when all three sisters came together. I knew that at some point there was going to be an explosion, because there always was. The dynamics of their relationships are complex, with so many different emotions and years of turmoil that has never been dealt with or even confronted until now. My wish for the three sisters is a healthy relationship that we can all share as a family.

It's hard to put the right words together to make you really understand what kind of person my Grandma Bonnie was. She made you want to be a better person. I often wonder what my life would be like today if she were still here, what different paths I would have chosen. Most often, I wonder if she would be proud of the person that I have become. She had big plans for me, you know; she had me choosing careers and picking out colleges when I was in the sixth grade. I loved her so much. She was always happy; she always had a song to sing; and of course, she spoiled me rotten, too. I spent so much time with Grandma, especially in the summers, when Mom was working. She taught me to sew and how to be a lady—and oh, how she loved the Lord. She lived her life for God, and she loved every minute of it.

Grandpa always had a joke and a nickname for everything and everyone. My grandpa Larry has to be the smartest person I have ever known. The way my grandparents loved each other and everyone around them was phenomenal; it could just swallow you up in its warmth. They held people to a higher standard, just because the thought of disappointing them was unthinkable. I know they did not like my father, and I know they were not happy when they were told about my being "on the way." Decisions were made and plans were set into motion to allow me the best life that they could give me. I was accepted into the family as any grandchild would be, with open arms full of love.

Sometimes I feel as if I've been robbed of the memories of the only time when my family was my mom and dad together. I look at the pictures from those times and wish so hard that I could remember. I am sure this is normal for most people. Those pictures are my only link to how my life began, and they are my most prized possession. Without them it's as though it never happened. My mom and dad have always been civil with each other; they never spoke badly of one another to me. Yet, to me, it's as though they were never together and those times are only stories and pictures in a book.

I do remember moving to the farm when Mom married Patrick, and I remember how much I loved all the animals; I think we were happy there in the beginning. One day they sat me down and told me that I was going to have a little brother or sister. I do not think that I really understood how that was going to change things. After Adam was born, things changed for me in a big way; I was second fiddle in his father's eyes. One day when my brother was about two years old, Patrick got very upset with me. He said that I had almost shut Adam's fingers in the bathroom door. I remember him yelling at me; my mom was yelling at Patrick for yelling at me, and I ran and hid.

I think that I went to stay with my dad shortly after this for my normal weekend visit. When my mom came to get me, she was driving a different car than usual, I don't know why this struck me, but as soon as I saw that car I knew we were not going back to the farm. I was a very precocious child; I heard and understood a lot more than anyone gave me credit for. I knew that my brother was not with us, that we had to leave him at the farm, because Patrick and his family had threatened my mom with terrible things if she ever tried to take him away. I don't remember how that made me feel; I don't remember a great sense of being torn apart from him. Do I think that our being separated might have hurt or changed my relationship with my brother? However, those two years after my brother was born were very hard for me, and I had grown to fear Patrick.

Leaving the farm was more of a relief for me than a hardship; I think that may have overshadowed the fact that we had to leave Adam behind. I have never asked my brother how any of what happened then affected him. That is not a conversation that I'm ready to have just yet. We had a hard time getting along as kids, which was mostly my fault, I'm afraid. Like any little brother, he always wanted to be involved with everything I did, and like any older sister, I didn't want him to be. Was this because of the circumstances, or was it just our age difference and the way things are between siblings? I guess we will never know the answer to that. As adults we have a good relationship. As the years go by, our bond seems to grow stronger. I'm proud of my brother and the man that he has become.

Christina and Adam, my favorite picture

Adam – always hunting

Adam Holding his little buddy

It's a fact that everyone assumes that children who come from abuse will also be abusers. I am here to tell you that this is not true. My mother set out to prove everyone wrong, and she did. From my earliest memory, my mother has tried to protect me and shield me from our somewhat turbulent existence. I was an easy child in many ways; I didn't act out and didn't require a lot of discipline. The rules were set, and I knew what was expected of me: act like a lady, don't talk back, respect adults—easy enough. My mom could put me in line with a mere look—"the one-eyed look" is what I called it—that's really all she ever needed. For a long time it was just the two of us; then my brother would come on the alternate weekends.

Mom had her boyfriends; some would stay longer than others. Some were good and some were not; only one was terrible. Her goal was to protect me from everything that she had ever had to suffer, which she did and did well. She could not, however, protect me from everything. You cannot turn a child's love on and off like a faucet, bring a person into his or her life and tell the child to love that person. "He is our knight in shining armor," she would say to me almost every time she thought she had found Mr. Right. Then, when the relationship went bad—and it almost always went bad—they would just be gone. I would not allow myself to get attached to any of the men who came into the house, to love them one after the other and then get my heart broken when they were sent away.

They seldom ever left of their own free will. My mom has always had a way of finding the wrong man and convincing herself for a time that he is the one, overlooking his bad habits and accepting things that she knows she cannot stand in a relationship. Eventually, she wouldn't be able to stand putting up with those things any more, even though they were fine in the beginning, and she would start trying to change the rules of what was acceptable in the relationship. As you may well know, this never goes over very well. When they didn't change for her, they were, well, gone.

I learned to stop investing myself in people; I don't get attached and it doesn't hurt when they leave. I do not give my love freely. I am guarded; the wall that I have built to protect my heart is strong. Grandma had a way with my mom; she made sense of things when my mom couldn't see her way through. Grandma was her solid foundation to fall back on when things were too hard. Grandma kept her grounded and could always set her back on the right path if she fell off. All of our lives changed so greatly when Grandma got sick. Everyone thought that she was the strongest person in the world—she would beat this, and we would move on. That is not what happened. We lost the glue that held us all together, and in many ways our lives fell to pieces without her. I still grieve for her, and I dream of her. I cannot walk through their house without pain in my soul that she is not there. My Grandpa is a lost man without his Bonnie.

My mothers' rock is gone now, and the only foundation she has to fall back on is me. I was fourteen when Grandma passed away. Mom was married to Steve then; the marriage was rocky before Grandma got sick and got much worse after she died. The fighting got louder and more frequent. I started hearing the word divorce more and more often. I left for the summer to stay with my dad in Florida, thinking that things were rocky, but okay, at home.

One random Sunday night the phone rang. It was Mom, and all she said, very abruptly, was that she and Steve were getting divorced, and then she hung up. I did not want to go home. Life at my dad's was easy; all that was expected of me was to be a kid. I knew what was waiting for me at home. It was my choice; I could have stayed with my dad, but I knew that she needed me and that I was all she had. There was not really a choice; I had to go back to her.

It's hard to summarize an entire life on a few pages, but up until this point I had been a very sheltered and much-protected child. Yes, we had tough times, and things weren't always perfect, but we always had enough of everything. Looking back, I don't know how she managed to give me as much as she did. Life was very different when I came home that summer. I was no longer my mother's child—I was her friend, her confidante, her counselor, and her keeper. The rules were thrown out the window; I was free to do as I chose for the most part. We went out together, and the two of us got a lot of attention, which we both ate up. At first I didn't realize how much she was partying, because I was out just as much. As long as I was with a friend, she didn't seem to care what I was doing. If she knew what I was doing, she ignored it, and if she didn't know, she should have. We were both reckless, and neither one of us seemed to care; the problem was that I was only sixteen. This would seem to be every teenager's dream, but believe me, it wasn't! She was on an emotional roller coaster; one minute she was happy, and then she would get depressed, which usually ended up with a really bad drinking spell. It was like a never-ending cycle, almost as if she were terrified to not have someone. It got worse when I met someone; I started spending time with and loving someone other than her. She knew that I was almost eighteen and that I was planning to move out. I know that she was scared of being alone. She was an emotional mess: she hadn't dealt with Grandma's death, her marriage had ended, and I was growing up so fast.

At times she was so depressed that she couldn't function. They called me from the bar one night and told me to come and get her. She locked herself in the bathroom when I got there and screamed through the door that she wasn't going to leave. The next day I took her to the doctor, who drugged her out of her mind on antidepressants—a big help that was. I felt trapped. I was the mother of an out-of-control, depressed, and drugged mother. After high school I moved out—or should I say Mom sold our house and moved in with someone. I will never forget that first night in my apartment; it's what I had wanted so badly for so long, to be on my own. Then why did I feel as if I had just abandoned my own child? I cried myself to sleep, worrying about where she was, if she was safe, and if she would be okay without me.

For a few years, we did the same dance over and over. If she was in a relationship, she was okay, and I could breathe. When she wasn't, I was always on edge, wondering what was going to happen next—there was always unrest. Then there was the worst night of my life. Things changed after that. That night, she called me from a bar, and I could tell she was drunk, so I went to get her. I wasn't mad. I just wanted her to come home with me. She thought I was mad, so she decided to drive herself home. There was nothing I could do to stop her; all I could do was follow her to make sure she got somewhere safe. It was snowing really hard, and she was swerving all over the road. I tried to get her to pull over, but that only made her go faster. She wrecked right in front of me—she could have died right before my eyes! She could have killed innocent people. I don't know how, but it was a minor accident, and everyone was okay. She was out of her mind and threatened to kill herself. I had to decide what to do with her: whether to send her to jail, send her to the psych ward, or take her home with me,

I needed help. I needed to show someone who cared what was happening, someone who would have influence over her. I wanted Grandpa, but I couldn't bear to hurt him like that. I got an old friend, Robert, and his wife, and of course Sherri, Mom's best friend. They all tried to talk to her, but she wouldn't listen; of course she felt it wasn't her fault. For the first time in my life I stood up to her. She wanted me to help her get out of the charges, and I said no. She really didn't understand what she had put me through; she could not see past her own nose. She almost destroyed us, our relationship, that night; I could not forgive her.

We didn't speak for months. I do not know if she ever really understood what she did to me that night, but things changed after that. She called me one day and asked me to lunch, and we never spoke of it again. We changed after that; somehow I think it brought us closer as mother and daughter. I was no longer my mother's keeper. After that we started to build the relationship that I cherish today. We might never have gotten to where we are now without going through the times we did together.

Our lives make us who we are, and we are two very strong women who will fight tooth and nail to get what we want in life. And we will always fight together, side by side, as mother and daughter. Life is hard. When I look back I see a bumpy road, but I do not see horror or tragedy. What I see is a woman who raised a daughter the best she could. My mother has her faults, just like everyone else. She did not get everything perfect—what parent does?

Now that you know all about what she is not, let me tell you about who my mother is. My mother is a strong, independent woman who lights up the room with her personality. My mother loves me—do you want to know how I know that? She tells me every day, every time that I talk to her, in fact. She built a great life out of nothing, and she shares it with everyone around her. I told her it was time to find a place to settle down. She has a grandchild now, and we need a place to have a Christmas tree and be a family. When she decided to buy her first home, she described what she wanted, and I found it for her. We stood in the driveway, and I knew that she had already made up her mind to buy the house before we even went inside. She tells everyone that I found her dream home. We have our own little family, and we build an extended family every holiday out of people who have no family to go home to.

Okay—enough about Paula, Paula, Paula! I want to talk about Christina! I met a boy when I was sixteen, and we have been together ever since. By the time I graduated from college, we had been together for ten years and decided to get married. The only person that I could see standing beside me as my matron of honor was my mom. So I graduated from nursing school on a Friday and got married the following Sunday. I want to tell everyone about the greatest week of my life. My dad came home the day before my graduation and stayed until after the wedding. My dad was newly single, and so was my mom—not that I thought that they would get back together, but I had them both together, and they were all mine. We ate together, we laughed together, and we did everything as a family. For that week I got my wish, and I loved it. On that Sunday in June, my daddy gave me away, and I married my love, with my mom at my side. It was the most perfect day of my life.

Chapter 17
Hundreds of Miles and Rose Bud

The writing of this story has been a labor of love. I have relived over thirty years of my life, in the form of a memoir. My life began as the first of five girls. I lost my mother at a young age, and I navigated through being adopted and in and out of seven different foster homes after abruptly being separated from my siblings.

My greatest fear in releasing this story was that the reader would put this memoir down with sadness or would perhaps experience anger at knowing so many children were hurt and traumatized throughout my story. My biggest wish is that you come away from this story knowing I have overcome adversity with a master's degree in the school of hard knocks, and I still have a smile my face.

The intense details of this story are told in my voice, to allow the reader to take a journey inside a former foster child's mind, to understand her fears and tears, and most of all, her struggles. I am pleased to report that through the last twenty-five years struggling in and out of this story, I have risen above a multitude of remaining adversities. The difference is that I now understand that the struggles were unthinkable then and today. Years of constantly reliving the painful and unkind memories have allowed me to achieve peace within myself, understanding that it will never really go away. As a former child of adversity, I now know that I have a choice as to how I react when these memories rise within me. As I travel as a keynote speaker in and out of different groups of youth, both in and out of adversity, I know from the expressions on their faces that I have made the right choice in turning this story into an instrument to give hope to those that need it. This writing has become the closing of one chapter and the opening of a whole new journey, which I embrace.

Adults growing up through adversity never like to admit that these memories affect them for their entire lives. When you pretend to be free from the past and don't deal with it, it can only leave scars that damage your psyche. When you don't gain this knowledge, it is too easy to ask for something to numb the pain or drink it away. My whole journey was all about asking questions during past struggles and learning how to take the answers and direct them into a positive direction. No matter what your background, my greatest wish in sharing this story is that you see strength, not sorrow.

I have a great deal of admiration and respect for any caseworker whom has the desire to make a difference in a child's life. These kids remember every kind word and generous act. You are the first person they encounter as they come out of their painful and hurtful worlds and into their new world of the foster-care system. As a former foster child who had roughly a dozen caseworkers throughout my journey, I can tell you that without the little talks and pats on the shoulders, this memoir and the telling of this story would not have happened. While foster parents have their hands full just loving each child and blending them into their families as their own, you as caseworkers   have a unique position with the youth to give them enough guidance during your visits to help them understand that they are no longer victims. Just a few of my caseworkers: Buffy Fisher, Sondra Rowlands, Betsy Nixon, Paul Gideon, Helen Smith—but most of all Judith Goodhand—did just that.

Foster and adoptive parents, it takes a true heart of gold to open your homes, hold onto your marriages and your own kids, and then let's add staying up to date with all the rules that are involved with today's fostering/adopting systems. You are angels sent in disguise when you open your homes to someone else's children. Not just anyone can learn to love a child that has had unspeakable crimes committed against him or her. I am sure there will be a special place in heaven for all of you angels. I am almost certain that Bonnie Ulrey will be among your welcoming committee. As a former daughter of seven different foster homes, I tell you that you do matter a great deal more than most of you will ever know. Each and every act of love will slowly edge away the pain for these children. Most of you will never know how much you are appreciated. I know that the constant replaying of your kindness in their minds will replace and push all of their unthinkable memories to the back. It will take some of these kids much longer to get these videos pushed to the back, depending on the amount of trauma they suffered before entering the system. For most, the offer of your commitment and home is the most generous thing they will ever know. You do have support groups within your counties and online. Here are just a few:

www.fosterparenting.com/foster-care/support-groups.html
www.lcsnw.org/ffk/support.html
www.dailystrength.org/c/Foster-Care/support-group
www.fostercares.org/

Are you thinking about becoming a foster or adoptive parent? You are not going to be perfect—no one is. If you have a desire to make a difference in a child's life, this message is for you. When I was finishing the last chapter of this memoir, I called Larry and asked his wise advice about making a training video. I wanted to put together a training video for some of the foster-care workshop events and keynote speaking events for the future, since it was getting harder and harder for him to get out and travel with me.

The question was going to be: "Why did you and Bonnie decide to become foster parents in the seventies?" I was totally caught off-guard and stunned at the revelation that happened during the filming of this video. Up until this day I had believed that, as much as we had talked about his days as a foster parent, I knew everything he felt about this subject.

When I first arrived, he knew ahead of time what we were going to be doing, so he shaved and put on his favorite fleece sport shirt. He chose the place we would set up the video. He wanted to sit in his recliner, the same one that Bonnie had bought him back in the seventies. The recliner was positioned in Bonnie's little study. He had his blanket over his knees, and I remember it being so cold that day that I was shivering through the whole filming. I positioned myself about six feet away from him. I remember being jolted with chills when I looked through the camera that day to see all of Bonnie's books still positioned on the shelves behind the recliner, just where she had left them.

Larry seemed unusually nervous. By now he was comfortable with a camera in his face and me blasting questions away at him. He was always ready to film; it made him feel as if he could still help "the kids." Today was different. He was just unusually touchy and nervous. We had stopped a million times, when he blurted out for me to go home and come back the next morning.

When I arrived the next morning, we had a bit of breakfast before we began the filming again. While we were finishing our breakfast, he told me that he had sat up all night to make sure this answer was perfect. It was as if he had been waiting for this question for years. He also knew me well enough to know that this was one of the most important videos we would make together. This would be his voice to the new foster parents of today.

The answer was orchestrated well on the video. It went something like this: "Bonnie and I knew in the seventies that there was a push to get kids out of the institutional living environments, and we wanted to help this cause. We took all the training and became licensed. All of our kids left soon after graduating and were off and married, leaving the house empty and quiet. My biggest reason for becoming a foster parent was because I do not believe that I connected to my four birth children as a good father should. I believe that I was average at parenting and that Bonnie was brilliant. My reason for wanting to be a foster parent is that I wanted a second chance to become a better parent than I was to my birth children."

As I held the camera and listened to this, it was like Niagara Falls letting loose on my side of the camera. If you ask me, his yearning for a chance to be a better parent was my blessing. He more than accomplished his goal, and he says that if they would still give him kids, he would keep filling that old farmhouse with more children. At his age of eighty-seven years, he never looks back with regret at his generous commitment and love for so many children.

If you are a former or current foster child reading this memoir, I already know that you read the words as if you own this story yourself. Most of you say to me "it's if you already know what

I'm thinking.". I know this because I have visited over a thousand of you over the last two years, and your questions and remarks are amazing to me. My message to all of you is simple and goes something like my favorite quote: "Life isn't about waiting for the storm to pass; it's about learning how to dance in the rain."

Adversity makes us strong and versatile. We learn from incredible people to take care of ourselves in every area of our lives. We reach out and appreciate each person involved in our lives and appreciate their kindness in our world of change. Our biggest job is to break the cycle of abuse when raising our own children and never to allow our children to live through our past. Most of all, we need to throw away the idea that our past trauma makes us victims for the rest of our lives.

Today, the era of computers, we research and find answers to our questions and struggles. Most of all, we try to make our adversities a positive vehicle reaching out and watching out for the youth that are coming from the same situations we did. I invite you to visit my website at www.edgeofunthinkable.com. If you are looking for support from other foster kids or clubs, please go to these websites: www.fosterclub.com or www.findingdulcinea. com/. My greatest wish for all of you is simply that you have *hope*. There are very few positive outcomes from the foster-care system, and I believe that we can make this number much larger. As former foster children, we must stop being victims of our past.

Overcoming adversity has built my character and given me the strength to stand before thousands to make a difference in a broken system. It has been an honor and pleasure to donate my story as an instrument of hope to help kids of today that are wearing what were once my shoes. Without being able to share the legend of my Larry and Bonnie, and of course, Judith Goodhand herself, I couldn't have told this positive story of how foster care has a great potential to save children that seem beyond saving. While many view foster children as damaged and injured, these three people understood that they just need love and nurturing. They helped them without labeling them as damaged goods. Their love and commitment gave new meaning to the foster-care system. Judith Goodhand made a very common comment when she said, "If we could clone Larry and Bonnie Ulrey, we would have a perfect foster-care system." She was still quoting these words in 2007 during my last visit. Larry and Bonnie's part in this story has been called a road map for foster parents.

Who would have thought that through this journey I would have the opportunity to own my fantasy dream home? Larry encouraged me to never give up on my dream home. Most of all, he taught me to dream and to work hard to achieve the goals I set in life. I bought my little cabin in the woods at the age of forty-two years, and I share it with my family and friends. Now that includes foster parents and foster kids. My hope is to have this little paradise turned into a foster-parent retreat.

My little cabin in the woods, my paradise

Always blissful at the cabin

Today, my most treasured activity is spending time with my three grandchildren. My grandson is a ball of energy, just like his daddy was at the age of two. My little granddaughters (eight and four) are my second chance to watch sisters grow together, this time with no life interruptions. What a heavenly gift it is to be a part of this and to watch them grow together as siblings should.

I hope and pray that in sharing this story I show my readers that children experiencing adversity can rise above it and achieve all of their hopes and dreams in life. As I completed the writing of this story, it was a great form of therapy for me.

Today this story can be handed to each youth, parent, and case manager, to help them understand the inside perspective of a former foster child and ward of the state. My story includes the things that were successful and the things that failed. It also depicts the separation of a sibling group. It talks to youth who today experience bullying. My subtopic for speaking events will now be bullying.

Many people may wonder what leftovers or handicaps might remain in my life after I had written this story. My answer has been this: *a trust factor* in relationships. I have finally reached the top of that mountain. It has been a very steep climb!

I met my prince at the age of fifty. His name is Richard, or Rich. He says that God made his mold, threw it in the corner, and six years later decided to make me out of the same mold to be his partner. We are quite a complete pair, and now, I am so happy to say, I finally feel the concept of contentment. I did not know that word existed in my vocabulary—or quite honestly, that it *didn't*. Rich and I both knew, the moment we stepped up on the doorstep of the restaurant where we met, that our searches for oneness were over. This prince even came with two white horses! We are soul mates, the one-of-a-kind ones that you usually only read about and never get to meet. Our instant chemistry was like lightning. I believe in my soul, at the age of fifty, and I believe that Rich and I will live out the rest of our lives in happiness.

Who would have thought I would meet a prince at 50?

One of the subjects I talked on lightly in a previous chapter was how Larry and Bonnie knew that I needed more than the average therapy to help bring me back from the destructive and unspeakable place I was in. They allowed me to have my very own horse when I was fourteen. His name was Rose Bud or, as I called him, Buddy. Larry and Bonnie were light years ahead in the concept of equine therapy, and they allowed me this healing privilege.

About two months ago, I rode along with Rich to see a friend of his in a small town nearby. When we drove down the lane, I saw this magnificent black horse standing alone in a small field. I was instantly drawn to her, and Rich knew it. I stayed in the truck while he stepped out to chat with his friend. I found myself staring at this beautiful creature, and no matter how I tried to look away, my eyes were fixed on her beauty.

When Rich returned to the truck, he gave me this cute little smile and whispered to me that she was for sale. He had known before his feet hit the ground what I was feeling about her. It was as if he felt my thoughts from just sitting beside me in that truck.

I was awestruck by her beauty. I wanted to cry, and yet I could not let myself get my hopes up. Until this second, I had not considered that I might own another horse.

The words "she's for sale" were his way of saying, "It's okay to want her—go ahead and feel it." It wasn't something I'd thought about, but suddenly it was a possibility. The tears welled up inside me, along with the giddiness I had not felt since Larry had assured me so many years ago that I could have my own horse. I turned to avoid the tears, but they fell by the bucketful onto my lap and left me more than speechless for the remainder of the ride home.

Rich's friend came out to the farm the next day to trim the hoofs of Rich's three other horses. We asked a million questions about the black mare, and he suggested that I come back to his place to meet her and to take a short ride. I was awake that whole night; I couldn't wait to meet and ride this beautiful horse!

Morning finally came, and it was pouring down rain. That did not stop us from going out. When we arrived, Rich's friend brought her out of the field to meet us. The first thing I noticed was the size of her hooves and how much they splashed water every time they hit the ground—they were enormous! When she stopped in front of me, I was speechless at her size and her beauty. My first horse had been as white as snow, and this gentle giant was as black as Black Beauty herself. Immediately I felt the gentleness from her. Her eyes were soft and yet cautious. Without knowing her past, I felt we had something in common from the first eye contact. The owner explained that he had rescued her from slaughter, and they had nursed her back to health over the last year.

I loved her from the moment I reached out and touched her soft nose. My only regret is that I forgot the apples I had set aside for her. She showed her intelligence and seemed to be searching for a treat. I wanted to ride her immediately. She was so tall (eighteen hands) that I had to stand on the tailgate of a truck to get on her. It continued to pour down rain, but that did not stop me. I remember wanting to smell her horse aroma. The memory of Buddy's chemistry has never gone away; it was so distinct that I couldn't wait to smell the familiar horse aroma. Being wet from the rain, she had a distinct aroma so intense that it brought back instant fond memories from so many years ago. She had an expression that was inviting and trusting. The owner did not have a bridal for her, which frightened me a little at first. He told me I did not need one, as he jumped up on her and then stood up on her back to prove that she was all that she appeared to be. My first ride was with a halter and two leads and no saddle.

First meeting with Rosey, such a gentle spirit

The rain was steady and warm, and she was so careful not to slip in the mud. It became hard to tell the difference between my tears and the raindrops. What an emotionally cleansing ride! There is truly something to be said about equine therapy for those who love these beautiful animals. It was immediately clear that I had to have this new friend, although I still did not believe it was possible. I rode her away from the group so that they did not see me crying. I had not felt that young and energetic for many years. This horse had to be mine!

When I took her back to the group, I did not even have to tell Rich of my decision. He knew from the look on my face. The next words out of his mouth were, "When can you deliver her?" I was soaked from head to toe, but my heart was warm, and the feelings were a little hard to express. Yet I knew I felt *free*—I have looked for that freedom my whole life!

I do not think I can put into words how it felt to know that I would have another special, spiritual horse friend. I remembered how sacred it had felt to own my own horse in a world of uncertainty, when I'd lived in the foster-care world. Looking back, I remember those days spent riding Buddy as being much more than therapy.

I found myself in a daze for hours. Rich was so happy knowing that I was happy—you would have thought it was him getting a new friend. Since the day we'd met, he's always been able to articulate his happiness for me with precision. It is as if he can see straight into my heart before I even know what I am thinking or feeling.

They delivered my new horse to Rich's farm two days later. When the trailer came down the driveway, my granddaughter and I had been sitting there for over two hours waiting for her. I had asked my oldest granddaughter to be there as a part of the festive delivery. When it was time to back my new friend out of the trailer, she came out back end first. When she was finally out, she looked up and around at the farm that would be her new home. Her expression was so familiar that it brought instant tears to my eyes. Her eyes went from dark and troubled to calm and peaceful within moments. She knew she was home, just as I had known when I'd moved into Larry and Bonnie's home thirty-six years ago. The look of serenity in this black beauty was calming to my heart, especially since I knew that she had been a rescue project just one year prior.

Grandma and Raylene with newly arrived addition

New arrival

I couldn't wait to ride her, and I invited my granddaughter on the first ride. As Rich started the tractor for us to follow him on the beautiful paths in his woods, I asked my granddaughter: "Raylene, what should Grandma name her?"

Her words were exactly this: "Grandma, when you were young, you had a Rose Bud and he was a boy, so you named him Buddy; now you have a girl, and you should name her Rose Bud. Call her Rosey until she's an adult, and then call her Rose." It was final—she was officially Rose Bud, or Rosey.

1st Ride with Raylene, as she so tenderly named the new horse "Rose Bud"

After I launched this memoir to the world, one of my accomplishments has been to become a keynote speaker, not only locally, but statewide, and currently for national organizations. The audiences have grown to include those in the foster-care system, pregnancy-crisis services, colleges for social workers, high schools (to teach the plight of foster care), and the alternative schools. Within five months, I accepted with great pride an award for volunteering my services for the Public Children Services in Columbus, Ohio. The letter went something like this: "You have become a fresh force in the world of children's services …" Within a month after that, I signed a Life Rights contract, giving a screenwriter permission to write this story in the form of a movie.

My largest accomplishment has been to originate and conduct trainings and workshops for foster parents and case managers, keeping my voice as a former foster child, while instructing workshops using this story as an instrument of hope. Included, but not final, are: *Fostering: The Difference; Sibling Separation: Out of Sight, Not Out of Mind; A Foster Child: Misdirected, Redirected,* and *Receiving a Foster Child.*

My most humbling and honored experience through this project has been motivational speaking events for the youth themselves. I am thrilled to announce that a few recent trainings held for motivational youth include Rich as my partner. Rich's keynote revolves around his college experiences as well as his past experiences as a professional baseball player in the minor leagues. During his events, his positive attitude, energy, and knowledge encourage youth to dig deep into their dreams and to follow their passions into their careers. His knowledge and experience complement my keys, to help the youth overcome their past adversities as foster children. As my partner, Rich brings his own energy and successful knowledge to motivate the youth. I am happy to say that these workshops and events have been instructed in states such as New York, Ohio, Pennsylvania, and Kentucky, and the list grows each day. To see more on reviews from these workshops and speaking events, I invite you to visit my website at www.edgeofunthinkable.com

Paula and Rosey

Rosey and Raylene bonding

Reese and Rosey

Acknowledgments

First and foremost, a huge and humble thank-you to Judith Goodhand for encouraging me to share my story. In Judith's travels across the United States, she used this story to emphasize the importance of not separating siblings. For that, I applaud you, Judith, a million times. You embraced me under your wings, knowing that this story would be an instrument to help guide the kids of today who were wearing the shoes I once wore. You are, without a doubt, one of the special angel warriors who fought for all foster youth during the past fifty years.

Thank you to Dad, Larry, for your unconditional love and steady motivational words throughout this project. It was such an honor handing you the first memoir off the press. I'm fifty now, and you are still the same kind, loving dad you were from the minute you invited me into your family. Even though many years have passed, you seem to have become a legend: to so many foster parents, as a road map for their efforts, and to the kids to whom you demonstrate love through this story, no matter what. You are truly inspiring to so many families!

A million thanks go out to you, Kelly Bitner, for taking the pieces and parts that I compiled for over twenty years and helping bring this story to life.

Sherrie Trice, you came to my rescue over the span of twenty-five years while writing this memoir.

Sherri Trice – My most dearest friend

To my beautiful Christina, thank you for having the courage to be brutally honest. Even though you have never been a fan of this memoir, I believe your chapter has crumbled a wall between us. Your profound words in this chapter will not only be helpful others but have brought us to a place we otherwise could not be today. In Judith's words, "Christina's chapter was poetic to Larry and Bonnie as foster parents, and I cannot stop reading it." I know growing up as my daughter was never easy, but I would not trade one minute of our struggles, because today we stand strong and true as mother and daughter.

Paula- 25 years later what a journey,
and I have my new wings now!

Beautiful girl

Bella and first meeting

First meeting

Getting to know each other

Gotta Have Her

I think I'll name you Lady Bella

Lady Bella first walk about

New Team member

Okay, we like each other

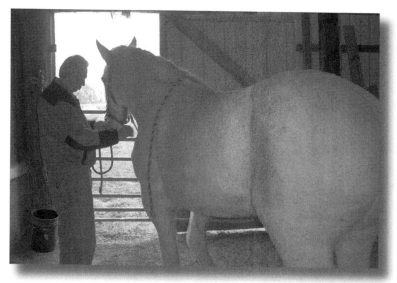

Rich and Bella's first meeting

Rich introducing Rosey to Bella

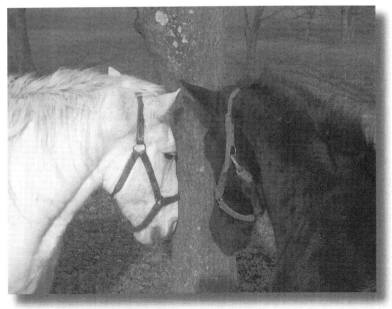

Well who's gonna be first

About the Author

Paula Kyle frequently speaks about her foster care experiences at trainings and workshops. She is a trainer with the Ohio Child Welfare Training Program. Kyle lives in a small town in Ohio and has two children and three grandchildren. Visit her online at www.edgeofunthinkable.com.